THROUGH DUST AND DARKNESS

THROUGH DUST AND DARKNESS

*A Motorcycle Journey of Fear and
Faith in the Middle East*

JEREMY KROEKER

RMB

Rocky Mountain Books
www.rmbooks.com

Library and Archives Canada Cataloguing in Publication

Kroeker, Jeremy, author
Through dust and darkness : a motorcycle journey of fear
and faith in the Middle East / Jeremy Kroeker.

Issued in print and electronic formats.
ISBN 978-1-927330-74-6 (pbk.).—ISBN 978-1-927330-75-3 (html).—
ISBN 978-1-927330-76-0 (pdf)

1. Kroeker, Jeremy—Travel—Iran. 2. Kroeker, Jeremy—Religion. 3. Motorcycling—
Iran. 4. Iran—Religious life and customs. 5. Iran—Description and travel. I. Title.

DS259.2.K76 2013   915.504'6   C2013-902648-7
C2013-902649-5

Front cover photo: On the road between Palmyra and Homs, Syria.

Printed in Canada

Rocky Mountain Books acknowledges the financial support for its publishing
program from the Government of Canada through the Canada Book Fund (CBF)
and the Canada Council for the Arts, and from the province of British Columbia
through the British Columbia Arts Council and the Book Publishing Tax Credit.

 Canadian Patrimoine
Heritage canadien
 Canada Council Conseil des Arts
for the Arts du Canada

 BRITISH COLUMBIA
ARTS COUNCIL
Supported by the Province of British Columbia

The interior pages of this book have been produced on 100% post-consumer
recycled paper, processed chlorine free and printed with vegetable-based dyes.

 MIX
Paper from
responsible sources
FSC
www.fsc.org   FSC® C016245

For my dad, who would ride through
hell if it would bring me home.

"We are doing the work of prophets without their gift … The fact is: I no longer believe in my infallibility. That is why I am lost."

Arthur Koestler, *Darkness at Noon*

ACKNOWLEDGEMENTS

First, I need to simultaneously thank and apologize to everyone who read an early draft of this book. Looking back, I don't know how you managed. So, here's me saying "thanks" and "I'm sorry" to David Miller and Jeremy Duncan, who were especially helpful.

Deborah Lantz slogged through several early drafts. She provided useful comments and fresh enthusiasm for the project with each read.

Ted Bishop, author of *Riding with Rilke*, gave me valuable feedback that made the book stronger.

Chris Becker read it too, but he only said, "Make it shorter."

Then there's Mark Richardson, author of *Zen and Now*. Mark gave the manuscript a basic line edit. Unfortunately, by that time in the process, I was tired. Mark's advice went mostly unheeded until another editor, Dinah Forbes, said much the same thing. And so I began another rewrite, with Dinah's help. Thank you both. Your insights shaped this book, and where it fails, it only does so in spots where I've ignored your advice ... again.

Several friends steered me away from selecting poor titles, such as, *And Iran. Iran So Far Away*. My second choice (for marketing purposes only) was *Another Justin Bieber Biography*. Shaking their heads at both ideas were the following people: Leighton Poidevin, Lynda Poidevin, Heath McCroy, Tom Wolfe, Mike Holton, Catherine Macdonell, Stuart Kroeker, Nevil Stow, Daryl Makk, Jordan Hasselmann, Sandra Hasselmann, Ekke Kok, Audrey Allenspach-Kok, Sands Musclow, Cindy Newton, and basically everyone who has ever heard of Horizons Unlimited (.com).

I have to thank several writers who have played either the mentor or the psychoanalyst in the past few years. In addition to those already mentioned, thanks to Matt Jackson (*The Canada Chronicles*), Michael J. Totten (*The Road to Fatima Gate*), Karsten Heuer (*Being Caribou*), Jerry Auld (*Hooker and Brown*), Stephen Legault (*The Slickrock Paradox*), Angie Abdou (*The Canterbury Trail*), and Jocey Asnong (*Nuptse and Lhotse in Nepal*).

Thanks to Scott Manktelow for designing maps, and to Jen Groundwater for the first round of copyediting.

Andrew Querner convinced me that the artist who suffers the longest wins.

Amanda Lindhout showed me what grace and forgiveness look like. Thanks for so many things, Amanda, but mostly I'm just glad you're home.

There's no delicate way to put this, but Nika Hubert put up with an incredible amount of BS. That's all I have to say about that. And thank you. (Oh, and by the way, there's more BS heading in your direction.)

This may be a little broad, but I really am thankful to fans of my first book, *Motorcycle Therapy*. Without your support and kind words, there would not have been a second effort. And without little independent stores like Canmore's Café Books, there would not have been so many supporters. So thanks to you too.

I'm grateful to Don Gorman and the team at Rocky Mountain Books, who carried this project the last mile. It was an eleventh-hour contract that rescued me from having to self-publish ... again. I really needed someone to believe in this story, as it was a difficult one for me to tell.

Thanks to many more friends that I just can't list – travellers, motorcycle riders, journalists, miscellaneous ne'er-do-wells – and thanks especially to my family.

My mom and dad may not appreciate or agree with some things that I've written, but they never failed to support me, and they are steadfast in love. I thought I was the luckiest kid in the world when they gave me my first dirt-bike, but I missed the point – I was lucky because they were my parents.

INTRODUCTION

The day's second call to prayer carried on a howling wind, reaching me through the engine noise before fading as I rode out of range. I shuddered. For the moment, the cool green of the Euphrates River Valley in Syria provided shelter from the storm, but all around me it looked as if God had chosen this space and time to dump out his vacuum cleaner bag. I looked up and noticed a small patch of dull blue sky directly above me. That, too, would soon disappear.

Plastic bags littered the landscape between ghostly towns, desperately clinging to whatever vegetation they could find to avoid getting carried off into Turkey, and sand drifted across the road like snow in a Canadian blizzard. The grit that ricocheted off my visor and silver helmet sounded like the static on an AM radio station during an electrical storm. Despite the fact that every inch of my body was covered with protective motorcycle apparel, a thick layer of dust coated my skin. I struggled to breathe. My eyes watered, the tears creating streaks of mud that ran down my cheeks and into my tangled red beard.

I could see the handlebars and instrument panel on my motorcycle. The speedometer indicated forty kilometres per hour. Beyond that, I could just make out two dotted lines on the grey road before me. That was my world.

But then, my path was obscure on a grander scale as well.

I had never intended to visit Syria in the first place. At some point on my journey I lost the way, and I continued now without a guide, without direction. Without purpose.

Out of the corner of my eye, I noticed the plodding silhouettes of a camel herd, stoic or oblivious to the desert's wrath. Then the storm, having given fair warning, blotted out every peripheral thing with an abrasive cloud of choking dust. I should have listened to the warning. Then again, if I had heeded warnings in the first place I never would have left home.

CHAPTER 1

The Greek mountains ended precisely at the border with Turkey. My passport slid back and a forth a few times to a worker on the other side of the glass before it had all the correct exit stamps, but it was routine. Soon I was back on my bike, riding across a narrow bridge over the Maritsa River. The river begins its journey in the mountains of Bulgaria. It spills eventually into the Aegean Sea, where it mixes with water that flows from nearly every country on earth, but at the point where I crossed, it's a dividing line.

Maybe the water doesn't quite divide continents – that task is left to the Bosporus in Istanbul – but it delineates political territory, at least. Crossing the bridge meant that I had arrived in the Middle East. That's what my map said, anyway.

The river marks a transition of cultures, too. In a way, it stands between the Christianity of Europe and the Islam of Middle East, but in today's world the lines between religions are not as crisp as the banks of some river. In fact, it was way back in Albania that I had heard my first Muslim call to prayer of the trip.

Even so, crossing that boundary meant something to me.

Flags at the midpoint of the bridge marked the spot where I actually left one country for another. There on one side was the blue-and-white Greek flag with a white cross, and the red-and-white Turkish flag with its white star and crescent was on the other. Primary colours and religious symbols, they all stretched out in a cold wind that day, snapping and tugging at white flagpoles.

It was the middle of October and I was bundled with insulating layers beneath my motorcycle riding gear, including an electric vest that plugged into my battery with a long wire.

When I got to Turkey I had to get an entry visa and buy insurance for the motorcycle. It felt like the first proper border crossing of the trip, even though I had already passed through half a dozen countries or so in the last two weeks.

I had shipped my bike from Canada to Germany. We had flown in on the same plane, the bike and I, and as I faced the carousel in Frankfurt, waiting for my checked baggage, I snickered at the thought of a KLR650 dropping down the conveyer belt. Instead, I had to get my bike from a cargo building the next day.

The German customs staff cleared my bike with staggering swiftness. The echo of the last rubber stamp to thump my paperwork had scarcely faded by the time I laid hands on my KLR.

Since then I had been in nearly constant motion to arrive here, at the frontier of another continent. And yet, as I rode into Turkey, everything looked familiar. There was a flat plain of brown grass pressed down by the wind, and every so often a small town beside the road. I might have mistaken the landscape for the Canadian Prairies, except there were mosques where rinks ought to be.

The road was straight and wide, allowing me to cover a lot of ground. I could have easily made it to Istanbul that same day, but there was no rush. The paperwork I needed for the next leg of my journey wasn't ready. It was there, in Istanbul, that I needed to collect a visa for Iran.

Why I had chosen to ride a motorcycle from Germany to Iran was a bit of a mystery, even to me. When people asked, I generally gave rehearsed answers. Iran is rich in history, I'd say. The hospitality of its people is world-renowned. I wanted to see for myself the nation that had been so vilified in the news in order to formulate my own opinion. After all, it was the summer of 2007 when I had decided to go, and I had left a few months later, in October. Back then, the President of the United States, George W. Bush, was in the latter half of his final term, and he was using some pretty incendiary language regarding Iran's nuclear ambitions. If the political vitriol between Iran and the West were to get any worse, then the window of opportunity to visit might soon slam shut. Ultimately, however, these were only partial truths.

The fact is there was something else about Iran that tugged at my heart. It was the idea of visiting a theocratic nation. A nation ruled by God. (Maybe that's why my visa application was taking so long.)

I was raised in a Mennonite family, so the notion of God factored prominently in my youth. I was born in the same Manitoba town that author Miriam Toews fictionalized (slightly) in *A Complicated Kindness*. In that book, an angst-ridden character called Nomi says, "Mennos are discouraged from going to the city, forty miles down the road, but are encouraged to travel to the remotest corners of Third World countries with barrels full of Gideon Bibles and hairnets." Quite right.

We weren't the Mennonites that people usually think of when they hear the word. That is to say, we weren't stereotypical. Yes, my hand still wraps more naturally around a shovel than it does the handle on a briefcase, but I did not grow up on a farm. No one in my family drove a buggy. None of us wore black suspenders or grew funny beards (except for my dad, but that was in the seventies, when everyone had funny beards). It's just that we subscribed to the particular brand of conservative Christian theology preached by the Mennonite church.

Then, when I was eight years old, my family moved to an even more exclusive Christian community on the campus of a Bible college in Saskatchewan. There I attended a Christian elementary school, a Christian high school, and finally a Christian college where I learned to think critically back to predetermined conclusions. Could anyone have been more indoctrinated into a Christian philosophy than me? Answer: no.

So I considered God a lot. In fact, for years I thought about little else. Recently, though, I had struggled to define my concept of the Divine. More accurately, I had stopped thinking about it altogether. There were too many unanswerable questions. Too many differing points of view that seemed equally invalid. The last time I examined my faith, I felt it was juvenile. I stopped at the brink of tossing it all away in favour of a mature attitude towards life – one without imaginary friends. I bought books by Christopher Hitchens and Richard Dawkins, but I lacked the courage to read them all the way through. The timing wasn't right for those ideas. I put them on the shelf for later, along with a Bible that I hadn't opened in years. That's where I left it all, unfinished books on the shelf, and God on the edge of my mind.

Though I failed to process any of this before making my decision, at least on some level I must have hoped that a journey to Iran, a nation ruled by God, would provide closure. Maybe it would even provide the catalyst I needed to finally abandon God. If nothing else, it would force the subject of faith to the foreground.

CHAPTER 2

Besides having to wait for paperwork in Istanbul, I was in no mood to push through a long ride that day because I was still a bit hungover from the night before, when I got tangled up with a Greek motorcycle club. After skirting the coastline along azure waters of the Mediterranean for hours, I had pulled over for a break at a disgusting location. This is sort of my trademark move, passing one idyllic spot after another before succumbing to exhaustion and landing on a big patch of ugly. I should write a guidebook: *The Ugly Parts of Beautiful Countries*.

If that book ever gets written, that spot in Greece will get four stars out of five. It was a gravel pullout with a view of nothing. It even featured an abandoned transport trailer that exuded the odour of rotting meat. Details like that are what make these places special.

As I munched on stale buns and runny Nutella, I heard the thumping of a loosely fitted piston with slappy valves. It sounded a lot like my bike. The racket came from a red KLE500, a smaller, European version of my machine. The rider turned to look at me as the bike flashed by, and I waved in greeting. Turning around, the rider pulled in to investigate – you don't see too many KLRs in Europe.

"You picked a great place to stop," said the rider as she took off her helmet to reveal soft, feminine features and long auburn hair.

"I wanted to see the *real* Greece," I said.

Elisavet introduced herself as a member of a motorcycle club in Xanthi. She was on her way to the clubhouse following a scenic route through the mountains.

"Would you like to join me?" she asked. "You will be our guest tonight at the clubhouse. You can sleep on the couches for free."

Elisa led me up through olive groves, past slender cypress trees, broad-leaved hazelnut trees, and to a vantage point with a sweeping view of the ocean. A marble quarry cut into the slopes above us shone like a city of ... well, marble. We continued along a grey road with crisp yellow lines that I never could have found without a guide. Even Elisa, with all her local knowledge, had to pull over for directions at several forks.

We pulled in to a roadside café that had three European sport bikes in the parking lot, where she introduced some members of the motorcycle club, the most memorable being Vasillie. Vasillie was a bald, barrel-chested man with a moustache thick enough to stop bullets and eyes black enough to cast a shadow on the devil's Corvette. With Elisa acting as interpreter, he introduced himself as "the Great Greek Lover," but when I learned that he owned a grocery store, I dubbed him "the Great Greek Grocer." Vassillie had a nasty bump on his head that he attributed to a recent motorcycle crash, but he wouldn't elaborate. I'll bet he dropped a box of lettuce on his head.

Vassillie and the others were eating appetizers and drinking water mixed liberally with *tsipouro*, a distilled alcohol that tastes like batteries. Plates of feta, salted fish, mixed greens, olives, and bread came to the table, each one accompanied by a tiny bottle of tsipouro.

Elisa asked about my impressions of Greece.

"Well, I really liked that gravel pullout where I met you," I said.

"No, seriously," she laughed.

"Actually, I haven't seen that much of Greece, to be honest," I told her. "I've only been here for one night at Edessa, and I'll probably be in Turkey tomorrow."

"Well, what did you think about the waterfalls in Edessa, then?" she asked.

"Waterfalls?" I said. "Um. I just stayed the night and rode off the next day."

"What?" Elisa exclaimed. "What's the matter, is someone chasing you?"

"Yeah," I replied. "Old Man Winter."

Eventually we rode to the clubhouse, where the Great Greek Grocer set up shop behind the bar, pouring one stiff drink after another for the entire night … and the night was young. I remember Elisa reading to us all from *Sit Down, Shut Up, and Hang On!: A Biker's Guide to Life,* like Wendy reading to the Lost Boys: "Young riders pick a destination and go. Old riders pick a direction and go." The last clear memory I have is following the Grocer out to the yard with a flashlight. There we tried to climb a huge tree (which, in the morning, turned out to be a short leafy shrub).

So, rather than push through my hangover, I took a hotel room in Tekirdag, a port city on the Sea of Marmara, about an hour west of Istanbul. In the morning, I found a restaurant near the hotel for breakfast, where a young Kurdish man with dark features and tanned skin took my order. He said his family wanted him to marry.

"In Turkey," he said, "if you're unmarried by your thirties, you're already past your expiration date. People think there's something wrong with you."

I told him I was thirty-four. "Much too young for marriage," I said.

I said the same thing to a pastor once, after he had finished preaching about the importance of humble sacrifice, and how humble he himself was, and how humble we all should be, just like him. Anyway, I said that I was too young to be married and he said that it was the only way to live free of sin, otherwise I would be a slave to lust. I said it was a sin to ensnare oneself in a bad marriage just because you want to have sex. But I didn't say any of that to the waiter.

There's a Turkish proverb that says coffee should be black as hell, strong as death, and sweet as love. The waiter brought me a small dose of something to fit that description, along with a basket of toast. He then cluttered the table with dishes of wrinkled black olives, smooth green olives, boiled eggs, feta, cucumbers and tomatoes.

When I had finished, I loaded up my bike and set out in the direction of Istanbul on a fast highway. The traffic became hectic as I approached the city. Following the example of other motorcycles, I split lanes in between rows of cars. It felt safer to speed past the traffic than to have it racing up behind me.

When I could I stole quick glances down at the map on my tank bag, but a map only works when you can deduce your current location. Besides, on paper, the bustling city of Istanbul appeared as a tiny brown dot. I remembered buying that map in Calgary. Then, the thought of navigating with the sun and a ridiculously large-scale map seemed like a great idea. *It'll be an adventure,* I thought. But now, weaving through an unfamiliar city, I wished I could travel back in time. With that power, I would do at least two things:

1. I would buy better maps, and 2. I would go find myself in that Calgary map store and beat the shit out of me.

I stopped where I could to get my bearings, squeezing up against metal guardrails as turbulent blasts of air from rushing traffic shook the bike. Finally I found a wider pull-out, where I hoped to figure out my location. I removed my helmet to give my maps a good look.

A female police officer stationed nearby stepped up to me, smiling. She looked at my maps before calling over her colleague to help. He only said one word.

"Go!" he yelled, waving his arms as if shooing off a stray dog.

When I didn't move, his eyes narrowed to slits in leathery skin.

"Go!" he yelled again, as if he had just thought of it.

He pointed down the road, while I sat there, gazing back at him with a blank expression.

"Go! Go!" He stepped closer.

"OK," I said, pointing to my map. "So, let me get this straight. You're telling me to," and here I raised my voice to imitate him, "Go! straight down this road?" I winked at the female cop who giggled, but quickly checked herself and shook her head.

The man: "GO!"

At this point, the officer motioned for his weapon. I assume he was bluffing, but I suddenly remembered *Midnight Express*.

"Yes. Thank you for your time," I said.

Just before merging back into traffic, I shouted, "You're just mad 'cause you lost your empire!" That seemed like a witty thing to say at the time, but now I don't get it.

With the Sea of Marmara on my right, I had an obvious feature to follow, but eventually I needed to turn inland to find a hotel. I stopped a few times for directions to Aya Sofia, a well-known landmark near where I wanted to go, but as I zeroed in on it, the road spun me around 180 degrees. I could not avoid the turn.

I could not avoid the turn, that is, unless I followed tram tracks along an otherwise pedestrian thoroughfare. Pulling over beside a large "No Entry" sign, I switched off my engine to ask a cab driver for directions.

The driver pointed down the tracks.

"But, the sign says 'No.'"

The driver understood. He pointed to his car, frowned, and shook his head.

"No!" he said. Then he pointed to my bike, smiled, and nodded. According to this driver, in Turkey, motorbikes go where they please. Unfortunately, I soon encountered a police officer with a more rigid interpretation of the law. He stood in my way, motioning at me to turn the bike around.

"But, Aya Sofia," I said, when I had ridden close enough for him to hear.

The officer sighed. He looked down the tracks and then back at me. He was on the fence about this call, I could tell.

I was so close to where I needed to go. If only I could convince this guy to let me pass. As a tourist, I find that you can play one of two cards in these situations. You can either project confidence in your decision, like John Wayne, or you can play all innocent, like Little Orphan Annie. In this case I waffled, thereby mishandling both cards. I snivelled with swagger, if such a thing is possible.

Whatever I did, it worked, because the officer stepped aside. I like to think that he pictured the Duke in a little red dress.

The smell of roasted lamb on a wood fire poured through my open helmet visor as I feathered the clutch down a busy pedestrian street along the tram tracks. Smooth cobblestones squeaked under my tires when I turned this way and that to avoid waiters with silver trays of tea or men seated at wooden shoeshine boxes. After a few blocks the road opened up onto a green, sun-warmed park with palm trees and fountains, nestled between two mosques.

Aya Sofia was on my left, a spreading structure with faded salmon-coloured plaster and lacklustre domes like oranges wrapped in tinfoil. Its minarets were gilded at the tips, but otherwise were mismatched shades of pink and grey.

The real beauty of Aya Sofia is inside, thanks to a cavernous domed ceiling that seemingly rests on invisible pillars, as though held aloft on the backs of angels. Upon completion in 537 CE, the dome would have echoed with Christian prayers for nearly a thousand years, until 1453, when it became a mosque and worshippers prayed in a different way. More recently it was secularized and turned into a museum, so now it only echoes with tourists gasping at the grandeur of the ceiling.

On my right stood the Blue Mosque with its elegant minarets of white stone. The building changed colour throughout the day like a mood ring for the city until, at night, it reflected steadfast golden light from electric bulbs. It was built in the early seventeenth century and has remained a functioning place of worship ever since.

I parked the bike on the sidewalk and set off on foot to find a pension, where I locked in for a three-night stay. It was the longest I had tarried since the trip began. After scuffing my luggage up three narrow flights of stairs, I had no desire to leave.

At any rate, I needed to stay in Istanbul to see about my visa. Also, it would be an opportunity to do some maintenance on the bike. I needed to change the oil and see about the problem in the front end. The bike had a dangerous wobble. That's why I called it the Oscillator. It could have been worse, though. Thanks to my mechanic, the wobble was the only problem that remained.

CHAPTER 3

Just a few months before setting off on this trip, I found my-self on the Canadian prairies, battling a powerful headwind on the ride from Saskatchewan to Alberta. The needle on my temperature gauge hovered dangerously near the red, but just when it seemed poised to cross the line, the radiator fan would click on with a reassuring whir to drop it back a few degrees. The wind pummelled the bike and me, pushing us around on the highway like a plastic bag in the breeze. Hot air snatched away the perspiration that dared comfort me in the dry heat.

The wind carried the smell of burning grass. Prairie fire. My eyes began watering long before the thick column of copper smoke came into view on the horizon. I rode to-wards the smoke for an hour before it seemed to get any closer. Then it enveloped me. Open flames licked the edge of the road, imbuing the haze with an orange glow. When I geared down to adjust for the poor visibility, my engine sputtered and died. I pulled in the clutch. In the sudden ab-sence of engine noise, I could hear the crunch of gravel be-neath my tires and the light crackling of burning grass as I coasted onto the shoulder.

I pushed the bike along the road, past a line of pickup trucks, volunteer fire department vehicles, and police cars that had stopped to fight the blaze. I pushed for over a kilometre until I found clean air and shade beneath a grove of cottonwood trees.

I laid my motorcycle jacket on the ground, reclined against one of the trees, and stared at my bike. I had just bought it a few days earlier, and this was my first test ride. It was a green 2001 Kawasaki KLR650 with a silver gas tank. The bike had black plastic panniers covered with stickers, and one chrome mirror scavenged from a 1982 Honda, cantilevered in place with a fraying bungee cord.

If you've never seen a KLR, just picture a lawn tractor with two wheels. Add a few signal lights and a set of handlebars, and there you have it. Its single-cylinder engine sounds like a lawn tractor, too, and it provides about the same amount of horsepower.

That's partly why I love these bikes, *because* they're so basic. From the bike's inception in 1987 until 2007, Kawasaki had changed the colour of the stickers and the plastic a few times, but they changed little else.

Thanks to such antiquated technology, as the old joke goes, when diagnosing a mechanical problem on a KLR you can break it down into two categories: small problems and large problems. To solve a small problem, hit the bike with a small hammer. For a large problem, use a large hammer.

Unfortunately, I didn't have a hammer. Also, I didn't really know how to diagnose mechanical problems, either. After staring at the bike for some time, I called my mechanic.

His name is Quy, which rhymes with "free," which is what it cost to have him work on my bike. Quy owned a small motorcycle shop in Calgary and he liked the idea of my trip. He offered to help for no other reason.

Quy moved to Canada from Vietnam at an early age, yet somehow retains an accent that makes his English nearly unintelligible. Couple this with a poor connection on a cell phone and you have a conversation that consists of me shouting only the most important words.

"Quy! My bike is broken! Gas on pants!"

Quy yelled instructions back, most of which I didn't understand through the static on the line. Before hanging up, though, I caught the gist of his message. I needed to loosen off a screw on my carburetor. Then – and I'm being completely serious – I needed to hit the carburetor with a hammer.

I borrowed some tools from a farm kid with cut-off sleeves and a green Roughriders hat who had stopped to help. Then I called Quy back. Back off the screw, he said. Allow the fuel to drain. Turn the screw back in. Wait. Tap the carburetor with a hammer.

The engine fired up and idled perfectly. I thanked Quy, returned the tools and took off down the highway. When I got home, Quy set about further hammering my KLR into shape.

In the evenings, I went over to his garage to help. To keep me out of the way, he gave me tasks like wiping grease from bolts and handing him tools. Even so, I noticed whenever he unbolted something from the bike to inspect it there would follow an uncomfortable pause before he muttered, "Oh, no."

"Oh, no? What does 'Oh, no' mean?" I'd say.

Then Quy would remember I was there. With that, he could usually manage a thin smile before averting his gaze to say, "OK. No problem." (This is why you're not allowed to watch mechanics work on your bike in the dealership.)

He always said there was no problem, but his eyes told the real truth. I had bought a lemon. A piece of junk. Quy was the only thing that stood between me and catastrophic mechanical failure, and time was running out. Neither one of us had anticipated the scope of repairs needed to make the bike roadworthy.

After watching him work long into the night on my battered machine, I thanked him once more before turning to leave. Quy stayed on, inspecting the bike further and prioritizing a list of repairs. I closed the door softly behind me, noting that he had just removed another component from the engine. The latch to the garage door snapped shut, but not in time to muffle the sound of one final "Oh, no."

Click.

CHAPTER 4

I lay in bed and listened to the city of Istanbul. I could hear the tram, the ding of its bell, and the rasping of steel wheels rolling on silver rails. The electric motor on the train had a musical hum and a flair for the dramatic, mimicking as it accelerated the opening notes from Wagner's "Ride of the Valkyries." Flatulent buses hissed as their modern air suspensions struggled to compensate for a load of tourists and all the vagaries of a cobblestone road. All this, plus a curious layer of beeps, buzzes, and whistles emanating from various emergency vehicles, combined to create a symphony of sound effects. I envisioned Istanbul having transformed overnight into a pyramid of blocks, now hosting the world's largest game of Q*Bert.

But one sound transcended it all when, five times a day, the muezzin from the Blue Mosque sang his adhan. The Muslim call to prayer is like the church bell of the Middle East, only the call goes further than any inarticulate bell. It attests to the character of God and bears witness that Mohammed is his prophet. It implores the faithful to make haste towards prayer. The Sunni version even offers a friendly reminder during the pre-dawn call that "Prayer is better than sleep."

To the Western traveller, the adhan is a novelty – a thrilling reminder that the listener is exploring an unfamiliar land. Most describe it as beautiful, or at the very least, interesting.

Of course, that's an easy attitude to maintain if they are in the region on a two-week holiday. Any longer and the thrill begins to fade. Ears no longer perk up at the first crackle of the loudspeaker. Smiles wilt, and eventually people develop the ability to ignore the call altogether. That's easier than developing the habit of prayer.

It was a different story, though, when the muezzin from the Blue Mosque delivered the adhan. He defied even the most apathetic tourist to ignore him. His cry settled upon Istanbul like a blanket of serenity, smothering beneath its folds the din of the city.

Five times a day that call spoke to me. By the simple merits of beauty it challenged me to take up the Muslim faith. Yes, but it never called *me* to pray – at least, not to pray within the Mosque itself. It called Muslims, and Muslims alone. During prayer, people from all other religions, seekers even, were banned from the site. So, after the adhan, I considered myself called to the next tourist attraction.

On most occasions this meant the Grand Bazaar. Now, without further cues from me, you might imagine bustling corridors stuffed with aromatic spices, bolts of bright cloth, stained-glass lamps and meerschaum pipes. Indeed, the Grand Bazaar has all of these things, but mostly it has tourist kitsch. It's like a ski-town shopping mall.

Where was the real filth of a Middle Eastern market, the stench of animal sweat and greed? Where were the unsanitary meat shops and suspect food vendors? The sad fact is that majority of the Grand Bazaar has had its edges hammered smooth over the years by millions of tourists.

It's clean. The corridors tend to be broad and straight, lit by a mixture of skylights and yellow electric bulbs. It has a food court with domed ceilings painted red, blue, and black. Bored merchants would rather smoke and sip tea than hawk and haggle. In other words, the Grand Bazaar lacks the annoying features of other Middle Eastern markets, and that disappointed me.

Seeking a more authentic experience, I wandered the few hundred metres from my hostel to the Blue Mosque one morning. I arrived just as the muezzin called out his adhan. Again, it made no sense to me how the wind could carry a voice so heavy with sorrow. The cry seemed laden with ancient tears; how could it hang there for so long? If it refused to sink, at least it should rain. As usual, the call froze me where I stood.

When it ended, I bought a cob of roasted corn sprinkled with coarse salt from a vendor in the square. I had to wait until prayers finished before I could enter the mosque.

After everyone finished their prayers, I removed my sandals and went in through a side door. With bare feet I padded along a soft red carpet into a vast room with four massive pillars. The pillars, graced with golden Arabic script on a blue band, held aloft an expansive dome. Sunlight sparkled through stained-glass windows, dancing upon the gilded text before settling in to warm the carpet.

Tour guides shepherded their flocks around, shouting out snippets of history. Many of them carried numbered flags, flapping them wildly to attract wayward group members. People jostled for the best position from which to scan the building with the LCD screens on their cameras. Flash bulbs popped in the cavernous room, effectively illuminating the first ten metres of a yawning depth of field.

I had my camera out, too, except I photographed the crowd. I struggled to reconcile the call to prayer with the tourist throng inside the mosque.

Of course, no one ever intended for these two things to connect. I know that once you remove the worshippers from a building you are left with just a building. Nothing is sacred that is not alive. Still, I had an awful feeling like none of this was real ... spirituality, religion, anything. It felt like a show, and all of it, every single version of it, seemed exactly the same.

I felt hollow. I felt foolish, as well. Sure, I had come to the Blue Mosque as a tourist, but to be honest I had also come because of the muezzin. His adhan had drawn me. Now, amidst a sea of nattering tourists, the holy mosque felt decidedly irreligious. I had burdened the adhan with my own meaning. I had validated it based on how it made me feel. I had given spiritual significance to pure aesthetics.

This is not to say that the muezzin lacked sincerity. Perhaps his song expressed a heartfelt desire to commune with God. Maybe. Or maybe the guy could just really sing. Either way, I had shirked my responsibility to filter an emotional response and analyze the underlying message. Was God really speaking to me five times a day through a call to prayer sung in a language that I did not understand? Or was the call simply captivating, with no particular meaning for me?

Rich Mullins, the late American Christian worship music composer, recalled an incident where someone approached him after a concert saying, "Wow! The Holy Spirit really moved at that certain part of the song."

The enraptured fan went on to explain the exact part of the song where the Holy Spirit did his thing, and Rich replied, "Well, actually, that's the part where the kick drum and bass come in." In other words, the same chills that wash over a congregation at the climax of "Amazing Grace" can occur in a cinema crowd at the climax to any movie starring Tom Hanks and Meg Ryan.

Heavy legs carried me back to the hostel. I dropped into

bed and lay there for hours listening to the city. Finally, the adhan from the Blue Mosque lifted my spirits enough that I could sit up. Then I left my room. Seeking an authentic experience, I wandered the Grand Bazaar.

CHAPTER 5

I had been trying to collect my Iranian visa for weeks before leaving Canada, but with the departure date looming, I was still empty-handed. I couldn't just postpone the trip, either. I had to leave before unbearable winter conditions choked off the mountain passes along Turkey's border with Iran. But by mid-September my bike still lay in pieces on Quy's workbench, and Quy had more bad news.

The aluminum swing arm was cracked. Quy had to remove the entire back end of the bike to get it welded. In doing so, he found serious damage to the rear wheel hub as well.

"Will the wheel be all right for a long trip?" I asked him.

Quy hesitated.

"Will you go over any bumps?" he asked.

"Yeah, probably."

"Well, OK. The rear wheel will probably be OK," he said. He knew that I couldn't afford to buy a new one. He also knew I didn't have time.

I had sat on the edge of my bed that night in Calgary, with my face buried in my hands. I didn't believe in omens. Besides, surely a motorcycle trip lacked the cosmic significance to warrant them. Yet, as I switched off the light, it occurred to me that a more superstitious version of myself would consider all of these little setbacks to be some kind of warning.

In the morning, though, things had started to change for the better. Someone from the Alberta DualSport Motorcycle Club had responded to my post on their online forum and agreed to lend me a wheel off his own bike. I still had no visa for Iran, but at least I got my passport back from the Iranian embassy in Ottawa. Quy installed the borrowed wheel and reassembled the bike just days before I had to bring it to the Calgary Airport. The night before delivery, I scurried around the basement, cramming armfuls of supplies into motorcycle luggage.

While packing, I considered how fickle "omens" tend to be. It all comes down to how one interprets everything.

Lost in thought, I had failed to acknowledge the dull ache at the base of my spine. Then, while lifting a heavy toolbox, I heard what sounded like someone wringing out a sheet of bubble wrap. It was my back. It had been bothering me for years following a construction accident, but I could usually deal with it. I didn't like the sound of those pops though. I dropped the box and stood for a moment, waiting for the pain.

Perhaps it clicked back into place after all these years, I thought, trying to fool myself.

The pain took its time.

Maybe that's the crack I needed. Maybe I'm cured. My mind returned to omens. *Maybe this is a good sign.*

The next morning I could barely move.

Forty-eight hours later I found myself drunk on a dirty cocktail of pain medication and jet lag, hobbling beneath the weight of an overstuffed duffle bag amidst the neon glow of Frankfurt's red light district.

I hadn't let the injury stop me, nor the lack of a visa. I would just have to collect it somewhere along the way. To help with that, I had found an agency online that specialized in organizing visas for Iran. The agency – let's call them the Incompetent Visa Agency – promised to have everything waiting for me in Istanbul. However, they had made no progress on my application by the time I got there. The simple procedure that they claimed would take ten business days had been ongoing for over a month. Deadlines had come and gone. Promises were broken.

Mahmoud, the agency's representative in Tehran, had answered my e-mails a month ago, when he wanted my business, but after receiving payment he stopped responding. When I switched from polite inquiries to hollow threats, Mahmoud finally replied.

"Your visa code will arrive within the week," he wrote.

I needed to collect an authorization code from the Incompetent Visa Agency via e-mail. Then, with code in hand, I would proceed to the predetermined Iranian embassy and make my application. So, I would have to apply again, but the code meant that approval was in the bag.

While waiting for the visa code to arrive in my inbox, I made some friends at the hostel. I left for dinner one evening with Dirk, a well-travelled schoolteacher from Germany. Dirk was on the youthful side of middle age, but his thin brown hair suggested that it already had plans to retire.

Following the tramline downhill, we passed restaurants and pubs and a little pastry shop filled with trays of sticky sweets and baklava speckled green with chopped pistachios. We made our way towards the flat waters of the Bosporus, a narrow strait that splits Istanbul in two, divides continents, and connects the Black Sea with the Sea of Marmara. We arrived at a broad path along the water. It teemed with pedestrians, food vendors and black-market salesmen selling dead batteries to ignorant people (I bought two packs).

The Galata Bridge spans the Bosporus, and we climbed stairs to its upper deck. Here, with their backs to the traffic, men with long fishing poles stood shoulder to shoulder against the blue iron railing, casting hooks into the water and pulling up small silver fish.

We walked behind the men, eventually descending another flight of stairs near the middle of the bridge to reach a pedestrian mall with a few good restaurants on the lower level, still well above the dark water. Although we could not afford to eat at a good restaurant, we settled into cushy chairs overlooking the river on the deck of a bar. Certainly we could afford a narghile and a mug of beer.

I was on a very tight budget. To pay for this trip I had sold most of my things, which didn't amount to much anyway. I had no home back in Canada, no reliable vehicle, and no job waiting for me when I returned. Actually, even this trip was partially funded with borrowed money. A friend had loaned me the cash to cover my carnet.

Carnet is short for Carnet de Passages en Douane. It's a document that allows you to temporarily import a vehicle into another country without paying extra fees. Essentially, it's a passport for your vehicle. I hadn't needed it in Europe, but I would use it in the Middle East. The problem is, to obtain this document, you place a cash deposit for a percentage of the bike's value with a motoring club such as the Canadian Automobile Association. The percentage is determined by the country you want to visit and one of the countries on my application required a deposit of 250 per cent the value of the bike. That's the main reason I bought a beat-up KLR. It had little value, and my deposit was only $8,000. The deposit would be refundable as long as I had a properly stamped carnet, or as long as I returned to Canada with the bike.

Our waiter returned carrying the water pipe by its long

silver neck. As he walked, he puffed on the wooden end of the flexible hose to stoke the tobacco. The pipe had a heavy base of hand-painted green glass and, as the man inhaled, the water bubbled happily within it, humidifying the velvety white smoke. Setting the pipe down on the ground next to our table, the waiter inserted a disposable plastic tip into the wooden mouthpiece before leaving once more to fetch our beer.

I took the mouthpiece and drew a long, deep breath through the hose. The smoke melted on my tongue like apple-flavoured cotton candy. It felt cool and soft as it flooded my lungs, where it remained for a moment before emerging again in a series of perfect smoke rings. I watched each one rise into the warm night air over the Bosporus. So desperately I wanted one of them to beat the odds somehow and survive the night. With luck, my little smoke ring might attach itself to an adhan in the morning and carry all the way to God.

Dirk's holiday ended and he returned to Germany. We had only spent a few days together, but I missed him like a dear friend. I think, too, I missed his motivation. With Dirk gone, I found it difficult to get out and see the town.

Just as well, I suppose. I needed to do some work on the bike. I took an afternoon to change oil on the Oscillator, creating in the process an ecological disaster when I used gasoline in a plastic bag to clean my filter. Feeling guilty about the puddle of fuel I had left to evaporate on the roof of the hostel, and having no desire to witness the death of any waterfowl to happen by, I retired to my room.

I have yet to perfect an environmentally friendly method of doing oil changes while on the road. Cleaning my reusable oil filter is only part of the problem. The next question is what to do with all that dirty oil. I always try to recycle it, but I'm under no delusions that it gets done.

Here in Istanbul, I brought the dirty oil back to the motorcycle shop. One of the employees there seemed to understand what I needed, but he just left the containers on the road outside the shop.

CHAPTER 6

A dozen mosquitoes in my room conspired to keep me awake most of the night. Every time I began drifting off, one of the little bastards would initiate a reconnaissance orbit around my bed. Like a Cessna with an engine fault, the lone scout sputtered in and out of earshot – now waiting silently, now buzzing closer, probing the darkness for its target. That sort of psychological torture would throw a Buddhist monk into a hissy fit.

Eventually, I figured out a solution: earplugs. I resigned myself to the stinging. I just didn't want to hear about it.

Of course, the earplugs were ineffective against the other pest on my mind that night: Mahmoud. He had promised to e-mail me the visa code in the morning, but he had said that before.

I had no contingency plan if I could not ride through Iran. I needed that visa. If the code did not arrive in my in-box, I would have to redraw my entire journey. That thought made me shudder … or it might have been the mosquito that landed softly on my cheek.

As expected, there was no visa code for me in the morning. Pursing my lips against an onslaught of curses, I pounded out an e-mail to Mahmoud in which I demanded a full refund. Then, spreading my maps out on the bed, I plotted my next move.

CHAPTER 7

As I was leaving the hostel to find supper, a Japanese girl introduced herself.

"My name is Chikako," she said. "I don't speak Engrish, but may I come arong?"

How could I say no to that? Chikako wore sweatpants and a baggy brown jacket that masked her form but, judging by her face, she was probably slender. She had plain features – so plain that when I looked at her directly it took my eyes a moment to focus.

In spite of the preamble, Chikako did speak English, and she provided excellent company. She had that accent, which made me smile. Also, when she referred to a physical landmark, her arm and index finger sprang out to stab the air in its direction. She failed to give warning before doing this and she never, ever shoulder-checked. One man ducked out just in time to save his eye.

Chikako guided us to a bank of restaurants off the tourist path that served inexpensive meals. Her eyes livened when she spotted her favourite dessert on the menu, and she wiggled in her seat when the waiter brought out two orders of *künefe*. I snapped a photo of the girl smiling down at a golden nest of pastry floating on warm syrup.

I looked at the display on the back of my camera. Funny. The girl in the photo appeared somewhat attractive. I looked up at Chikako in an effort to reconcile the image on the screen with the person in front of me. Nope. Still frumpy. She had a nice smile, though.

When the conversation turned to travel plans, I told her all about the visa problems I was facing. Chikako rummaged through her bag to produce her passport. Flipping through the pages, she triumphantly displayed a valid Iranian visa, but her smile quickly faded.

"I want to go to Iran," Chikako said, "but my parents worry. They think it is very dangerous."

"People always fear what they don't understand," I said, examining the visa.

"Yes, but a Japanese student was abducted in Iran a few days ago and it's on the news," she replied.

I hadn't heard about that.

"Well, there are certain places you want to avoid," I said, handing the passport back, "but generally, the security situation in Iran is fine."

"I know. Maybe my parents would feel better if I went with someone." Chikako batted her eyelashes at me.

"Yeah, well, I can't help you there. It seems impossible for Canadians to get approval from Tehran."

In fact, it was harder by far to enter Iran with a Canadian passport than it was with an American one. Even the Incompetent Visa Agency conceded that. Their website estimated the odds of a Canadian getting a tourist visa at 41 per cent, though a footnote claimed, "The results have been much bette [sic] for Canadians, recently."

"Why is it so hard for you?" asked Chikako, now picking at her dessert with a fork.

I sighed and gave her the story. Tensions between Tehran and Ottawa came to a head over an incident in 2003 involving a female Iranian-Canadian photojournalist named Zahra

Kazemi. Kazemi was taken into custody after a photo shoot outside of Iran's Evin Prison. She died in hospital a few days later.

According to one doctor who examined Kazemi after her death, the body showed evidence of brutal rape and beatings. At first, Iranian officials claimed the fifty-three-year-old died of a stroke while under interrogation, but later changed their story to say that she had died of a head injury resulting from an accidental fall. Later still, officials admitted that, yes, Kazemi died from a blow to the head.

Such mistreatment of a Canadian citizen drew harsh, albeit belated, criticism from Ottawa, but the Iranians never recognized Kazemi's dual citizenship. In fact, they seemed bemused by Canada's interest in the case. At any rate, they saw no reason to allow a Canadian observer when they brought a guard to trial over the affair on charges of "semi-intentional murder." Predictably, the guard was acquitted.

To complicate matters, at the apex of Canadian indignation over what they believed to be a miscarriage of justice, Canadian police officers in British Columbia shot and killed an Iranian national. An investigation concluded that the officers acted according to protocol, but the incident remains a strong candidate for the "Worst Timing Ever" award. One can understand Tehran's skepticism.

Since then, Iran and Canada have bandied accusations of human rights violations across the pond like a shuttlecock. Perhaps the Canadian ambassador to Iran is the most jet-lagged person on earth, living out of his suitcase in the process of either being withdrawn from or kicked out of Tehran.

"So, that's why it's hard for Canadians to get a tourist visa for Iran," I said.

Chikako nodded. "Governments argue rike chirdren," she said.

Of course, she was not the first person to make such an observation, although a torture-related death hardly qualifies as the subject of a childish argument. It's the tit-for-tat bit that seems juvenile.

Chikako was still considering my visa problem when the waiter came to clear the dishes. Suddenly she raised her eyebrows. She recommended a guidebook that might help – *The Border Directory*, she called it. She was adamant, suggesting it over and over.

I assumed that she meant a directory of visa services located at the border, but I had never heard of it. At any rate, I didn't think another guidebook would solve my problem. I murmured something noncommittal before changing the subject.

Leaving the restaurant, we joined the evening pedestrian traffic at the Galata Bridge. To warm my hands more than anything, I bought some roasted chestnuts in a white paper cone. The soft chestnuts slipped easily from their brown shells. I tossed the shells to the ground where they bounced and clicked and finally crunched underfoot as we strolled along the bridge deck. The breeze carried with it the aromatic smoke from strips of lamb or fish that sizzled on the grills of vendor carts. The carts were all steaming and glowing white from the light of their kerosene lanterns. At this late hour, men still stood side by side, pulling up small silver fish and dropping them into plastic pails.

Chikako reached in to the cone to retrieve a warm chestnut.

"Are you Christian?" she said.

"Why do you ask?" I replied, dodging the question for the moment.

"Because you're from the West," she said.

She went on to explain that she was a Buddhist. But she

claimed to be Buddhist in the same way that most Westerners were Christians – in name only.

"Most Japanese don't have rerigion," she said, "but God is arways on our minds."

I doubted whether she could speak with any authority for an entire nation. Still, I wondered if the West represented the flip side of that coin, where everyone had a religion but seldom thought about God. Of course, I had no authority, either.

"So, are you Christian?" she asked again.

I thought for a moment, and my hesitation felt strange. Once upon a time I would have replied that, yes, I am. Then I would have marched this girl down the biblical "Romans Road," a series of verses designed to expose a person's wretchedness before unveiling their singular hope – repentance to and forgiveness through Jesus Christ, forever and ever, amen.

It seemed just that simple once. But now ... I hadn't thought about such things for so long. I found myself scrambling to formulate and express an opinion simultaneously.

"Yes," I said, after a long pause. "But not only because I'm from the West," I continued. "I'm actually a Christian, I think ... though I don't claim to understand things as clearly as I once did."

"What do you mean?" Chikako asked.

I stammered. I started to explain, but stuttered to a halt and said I'd get back to her when I had a better idea of what to say. We continued walking along the bridge deck.

"Well," I said with a sigh, "I guess I feel inadequate when I think about God, like there's a rift between us. There has to be. Maybe I feel that way because that's what I've been taught since childhood, or maybe there's really a God, and there's really a rift. Anyway, I hope that my inadequacies can be overlooked because of what Jesus did. But, I sure don't know. In fact, it all seems quite unlikely."

A fraying thread of hope. That's all that remained for a God I once thought I knew. I liked to think that doubt was healthy. To quote Voltaire (not that I usually do that, but when I punched "certainty" into my computer, this came up), "Doubt is not a pleasant mental state, but certainty is a ridiculous one." Certainty is partly to blame for religious wars, especially certainty in a monotheistic religion, as Reza Aslan suggests in *No god but God:* "One could argue that the clash of monotheisms is the inevitable result of monotheism itself. Whereas a religion of many gods posits many myths to describe the human condition, a religion of one god tends to be monomythic; it not only rejects all other gods, it rejects all other explanations for God. If there is only one God, then there may be only one truth, and that can easily lead to bloody conflicts of irreconcilable absolutisms."

Even then, I'd say that monotheism isn't the problem so much as the kind of certainty I once had in the whole system. If more of us used words like "believe" and "hope" instead of "know," there would still be a surplus of people willing to die for God. That's fine. Hopefully, though, there would be a shortage of people willing to kill.

Facing the river, I leaned against the railing on the upper deck and rested my head on folded arms. Down in the dark I could hear water splashing against the pillars. Chikako leaned on the railing, too. Much of what I said to her was lost due to the language barrier. Never mind. Chikako seemed happy enough just to listen, and I didn't feel like I needed to convince her of anything.

We walked home. By the time we said goodnight to each other at the hostel, I could see that Chikako was beautiful.

CHAPTER 8

Volleys of rain hit the window like fistfuls of gravel flung at a pond. Of course. After a week of sunny weather in Istanbul, the day I planned to leave, there was a storm. I could have stayed longer, but when I noticed myself pacing the room like a caged animal insane with boredom, I knew I had better go. Besides, Istanbul had learned to slip its grubby hands into my pockets to steal out the biggest coins. Still, I dragged my feet while packing. I checked my e-mail one final time for the visa code, or for any response from Mahmoud. Nothing.

I picked my way down wet linoleum stairs with the last of my luggage and pushed through the door onto the cobbled street. I clicked the plastic panniers onto my bike and then, though still sweating from the move, I donned layers of warm clothing and rain gear.

Although I had walked extensively in the area in the past several days, it took two tries to find the proper exit for the Galata Bridge. Missing another exit later on, I executed a complete revolution of a stadium before locating street signs for Ankara and the way out of the city.

Rolling along the Bosporus Bridge, a wide span of pavement suspended from zigzagging cables, I passed a sign welcoming me to Asia. The Oscillator and I had just crossed into another continent. "And we rode here," I whispered to the bike.

Before leaving the hostel I had asked the owner for directions to Ankara.

"Will you be returning to Istanbul?" he asked.

"I don't plan on it," I said.

"I mean, ever. Will you ever, ever be back with your motorcycle?"

"Uh, no, I don't suppose I will," I said.

"OK. Then take the far left lane when you reach the Bosporus Bridge ... and don't stop."

Strange. Now it made sense as I approached the end of the bridge. The far left lane was an express lane. It had an automatic billing system for collecting tolls. Blowing through it triggered an alarm and spinning lights.

I looked around as if to say, "Does anyone else find that siren annoying?" I even cast a bewildered shrug with my free hand, but my other hand rolled on the throttle.

I peered through droplets of water on my visor. The landscape looked much like anywhere in Middle America, except there were olive trees scattered throughout the wheat fields. Higher up in the hills, the trees had turned an indecisive shade of yellowish green, and above that there was a light frosting of snow. I plugged in my electric vest at a quick roadside stop before the final push to Ankara.

Along the way, my mind drifted back to the conversation with Chikako. I could see her. As I fumbled to summarize my belief system, she gazed out over the dark water towards the Yeni Mosque and its domes. Illuminated from below, it looked like a mound of golden bubbles. She looked at a mosque, a symbol of Islam, but our conversation orbited around Christianity. Anyway, to a Buddhist, it's probably all the same.

"I remember seeing churches in Paris," she said. "They are so beautiful. But I don't think that's what he wanted."

"Who, Jesus?" I asked.

Chikako nodded.

"You're probably right," I said. "I think he would rather see us helping people, giving more to people in need … loving each other. It's just way easier to build churches than it is to love."

I thought, too, about her advice regarding that stupid guidebook, *The Border Directory*.

"*The Border Directory*," she kept repeating. "Why don't you just go Directory?" she said. Go directory. Wait. Had she ever explicitly called it a guidebook, or did I make that assumption? She did have that accent.

"Go to the border directly," she said. She wanted me to turn up at the border with Iran to see if I could get in. From then on I had to ride with an open visor because it kept fogging up when I started to giggle.

I parked the Oscillator near a plinth that held a proud statue of a military commander on a horse. The commander was Mustafa Kemal, an effective leader in World War One who later changed his name and is better known as Atatürk, or "Father Turk." Atatürk won important battles against the Allies, most notably in Gallipoli, and he may have been responsible for the first genocide of the twentieth century. The Armenian genocide is still controversial today. Many Turks deny that it happened, while Armenians claim that the Turks destroyed or expelled up to one million people.

After WWI, Atatürk became the president of Turkey and unified the people under a nationalist banner. He modernized it and more or less made Turkey what it is today, but he often did so by strong-arming his opponents and marginalizing ethnic minorities, such as the Kurds.

Before leaving to find a hotel, I left charge of my bike to

a withered old man with a hacking cough. How he intended to protect my belongings remains a mystery, but he did lay down an impressive moat of phlegm around the machine. Perhaps the most careless of thieves would slip on that.

As I examined my guidebook, an agitated crowd marched along the street. They seemed to be chanting angry slogans. They held a giant Turkish flag over their heads like an elementary school gym class would hold a parachute, but they obviously weren't having as much fun.

Several people stood by on the sidewalk and I asked one of them what was going on.

"They are angry about the PKK," said one man.

The PKK (Kurdistan Workers' Party) is an organized group of Kurds that, among other things, occasionally spill over from northern Iraq to ambush Turkish forces. They were much more actively violent in the eighties and nineties, but they had recently killed dozens of people – soldiers and civilians – inside Turkey. At the time of my visit, the Turkish government was holding a crisis meeting in Ankara to discuss a cross-border raid into Iraq.

Since the crowd and I were headed in the same direction, I followed along while trying to orient myself on my guidebook map.

Rounding the corner, the mob encountered a stone-faced row of Turkish police in dark uniforms, armed with batons and Plexiglas riot shields. I lowered my book. The two groups faced each other, the crowd chanting and pumping their fists in the air, while the police remained unflinching. To better photograph it all, I jumped up on a short wall overlooking the scene at the crowd's flank. From this angle, the best shots were of the riot squad. I snapped away with the full understanding that photographing police is at best taboo. It's often illegal.

In spite of all these stimuli, my attention shifted from the crowd to a pizza bun in my hand. As the crowd raged on, I nibbled at the bun while scanning the square for any sign of a cheap hotel. When I looked back at the protest, I found myself staring into the lenses of two photographers.

One of the men, a videographer, collected a few seconds of footage. As far as I could tell, he captured me eating a pizza bun. The still photographer dressed in black, on the other hand, snapped image after image of me through his telephoto lens. I couldn't see his face. He never lowered the camera. Who was this guy? He used a professional-grade Nikon and he had a cell phone clipped to his belt. Reporter. Why should he find me so interesting? OK, I probably jumped out from the crowd a bit because of my dripping-wet motorcycle clothing, but that wouldn't account for all the attention. Did he know something that I did not? Suddenly my pizza bun got a bit hard to swallow.

The shouting died down when a fresh row of reinforcements jogged into place to bolster the already formidable wall of cops. Tension evaporated and, as darkness loomed, I decided I had seen enough. I needed to find to a room.

Skirting the edge of the crowd that had already begun to disperse, I left the scene behind me. I didn't get far. A few steps out of view of the protest, three men pulled me aside.

A thick man in a beige suit sidled over to block my path. Another man, thin, tall, wearing dark clothes, swooped in next to me, and I felt the presence of a third man close behind. Badges flashed, then disappeared into coat pockets. I took a bite of my pizza bun.

"Passport," the thick man demanded.

I nodded and kneeled down to retrieve it from a leg wallet strapped to my calf.

The thin man grabbed me by the arm and moved me against the side of a building.

"Badges," I said. I hadn't gotten a good look when these guys flashed their identification earlier, but if they were going to lay hands on me I wanted to be certain of their authority. The men looked at each other, but all three of them produced their ID. I inspected each one in turn. Do you know how you can spot a fake Turkish police badge? No, neither do I.

"Passport," the thick man demanded again, but softer this time.

As I bent down to retrieve my papers, the same faceless photographer snapped more shots of me. I gave him a nod. He lowered the camera and nodded back.

I handed my passport over to the thick man and took another bite of the pizza bun. The men demanded to know the name of my hotel, but of course, even I didn't know that yet. I explained that I had just rolled into town when I stumbled upon the protest, but I don't think they understood. I expected them to confiscate, or at least to examine my camera, but they never did. Finally, they just lost interest in me and let me go.

CHAPTER 9

The acrid scent of stale cigarette smoke so permeated the carpet in my room that I awoke in the wee hours rubbing my eyes. I coaxed a few raspy swallows of water down my throat before sliding the window open to look down at the Oscillator. There it was in the parking lot, a lonely silver-and-green motorcycle against a pink concrete wall. I leaned over the sill into the cool night for a breath of clean air, but the city smelled of roofing tar.

I sat down on the bed and continued rubbing my eyes. Why had I come to Ankara? Even the guidebooks suggested that a person could make better use of their time in Turkey than to visit the capital.

Why had I come? I planned to visit the Iranian embassy to make an appeal, but I didn't expect that to work. Really I had come to get the ball rolling on papers for Syria, my only reasonable option if I hoped to slip the tightening noose of winter.

In the morning, I poured a red tea concentrate into a clear glass before topping it up with hot water. As the cup had no handle, I held it by the rim with my thumb and ring finger, taking careful sips until the tea cooled. Each swallow soothed my aching throat.

To obtain a Syrian visa, I needed a letter of introduction from the Canadian embassy. Passing through security, I stepped onto a patch of manicured Canadian soil and took a deep, contented breath. A maple tree with red leaves stood in the garden, and I soon collected a letter from a man named Smiley. He offered to type one up for Iran as well.

"Will that make any difference?" I asked.

"Not likely," he said. "But it can't hurt. By the way, I must warn you about Syria and parts of Turkey," he continued. "No matter how trustworthy you think someone might be, if they offer you something to drink, do not accept it." He went on to explain that several travellers had been drugged and robbed in this manner.

"But, some of the most rewarding travel experiences come from interacting with people and accepting hospitality," I said.

Smiley shrugged. "I just have to warn you. Ultimately it's your decision."

After covering his bases and collecting the fee, he slid the letters through a slot in the thick glass that separated us, and wished me luck on my trip.

It had taken the better part of a day to accomplish this. I walked down through the long shadows of a park nestled in a gully where the only sound was that of rustling leaves and my own footsteps. It marked the first time since my arrival in Ankara that I could not hear traffic. I lingered there for a while.

Returning to my room later that night, I cracked open a cold can of Efes and clicked on the television to find an English news station. My laptop came alive in the time it took me to finish half my beer, and I opened up my e-mail. There was a letter from Mahmoud.

"Dear Mr. Kroeker, congratulations! You have been approved for a visa by Tehran. Please proceed to the consulate in Istanbul with the attached visa code."

I stared at the computer for a really long time. Eventually I shut it down and cracked open another can of Efes.

CHAPTER 10

On the return trip to Istanbul, I became so inventive with my riding positions that I looked like a freestyle moto-cross rider too afraid to fly. I rode sidesaddle. I lay prone, Superman-style, with my legs tucked back over my panniers. I rested my feet up high on the hooks above the front signal lights. I did all this to mitigate the pain stabbing at my lower back. Clearly, pain and stress enjoyed a symbiotic relationship.

After reading the e-mail from Mahmoud I had agonized over the decision to return to Istanbul. It meant a long, dull retreat, but the real issue was that I believed Mahmoud to be a liar. Straight up. I had this horrible feeling that he had sent me an invalid code, just a bunch of numbers to shut me up. Then again, what if the code worked? If I didn't try, I would never stop wondering.

I approached the Bosporus Bridge with some apprehension, fearing that they might have recorded my license plate when I jumped the toll on the way out, but nothing came of it. I crossed the bridge without consequence, landing right back where I started, in Europe, as if I couldn't decide on which continent to visit. Rush hour had just begun when I reached city limits, and the flow of traffic pushed me about to all corners and across every bridge, some more than once. I even ended up back in Asia for a few dizzy moments. When

I saw Chikako later that evening, she tried to envision my route.

"When I came from Ankara on the bus," she said, "I used not the Garata Bridge, not the next one, but the one before that."

"Yeah, well, I used all three."

I spent the next several days in a muggy room filled with unhappy people at the Iranian consulate. No matter how hot or how thick the air, I kept my long-sleeved sweater on for modesty's sake, just like everyone else.

In the evenings I had supper with Chikako. On the first night, a Middle East correspondent from a Japanese newspaper joined us. A distinguished man with a dark suit jacket and beige pants, he seemed out of place in our budget hostel. In fact, he was. His usual hotel had no vacancy, perhaps due to an influx of reporters covering the cross-border raids into Iraq to root out the PKK. For whatever reason, he ended up slumming it with us for a few nights.

Though the man was well spoken and had a broad vocabulary, he had a thicker accent than Chikako. Unless I made regular contributions to the conversation, the two of them would natter away in Japanese. This might seem rude at first blush, but I understood. After speaking English every day to others who spoke it poorly, it must have felt like a cool drink of water to hear his native tongue.

After conferring with Chikako, the reporter selected from the menu an unappetizing mess of fish of the kind people haul up from the Bosporus. They lay on the plate with their mouths agape as if caught in a silent scream, their dead, unblinking eyes staring up at me. I should say that the fish appeared unappetizing to me, for in the time it took me to locate the smallest specimen, grasp it by the tail and place it headfirst into my mouth, Chikako and the reporter had devoured most of the rest. In fact, they slowed their pace to allow me a greater share in the bounty. I forced a weak smile and picked up the next smallest fish.

To gloss over the embarrassing silence I triggered with a gag reflex, I asked the reporter about his job. He told us of how the newspaper had moved his family to Cairo, and how he spent an astonishing amount of his life away from them on business trips.

"How does your wife feel about that?" I asked, still holding the fish like a cigarette on the edge of my peripheral vision.

"She understands that this is the job," he said.

There followed a pause so pronounced that I could no longer air out the fish without attracting attention. I placed it on my tongue, mimicking as I did a face that I hoped would synthesize a look of calm satisfaction.

Next the reporter lowered his voice and, picking his words carefully, he said, "The gods only give you two of three things – money, freedom, or status. I have money, and I have status. But I really envy you two with all your freedom."

It was Friday. The faithful lined up outside the mosques to pray in the midday sun on their own prayer mats. Only the men did this, apparently. In fact, I don't think I've ever seen a Muslim woman pray.

Friday is the Sunday of the Islamic world. In other words, even though the consulate in Istanbul was open, most government offices in Tehran were closed. To make matters worse, Monday happened to be Republic Day in Turkey. Republic Day commemorates the declaration of the republic under Atatürk in 1923. It's a national holiday, and that made for an extremely long weekend this year.

As for Mahmoud, after writing the note that prompted

my return to Istanbul he had fallen back to his reticent ways, avoiding phone calls and ignoring e-mails.

I arrived at the consulate early. Normally the security guard would frisk me and give a quick sweep with his metal detector, but he recognized me now. On this day he just smiled and held open the door. Aw, that's nice. We had become friends. Maybe later we'd go fishing off the Galata Bridge.

Entering the room, I pushed through a wall of hot air to take my place once more at the back of a long line. I recognized a few faces, too, fellow travellers who found themselves stymied for the moment in their attempt to get into Iran.

The Taiwanese man in front of me had also used the Incompetent Visa Agency. He dealt with Mahmoud, and he received his confirmation e-mail the same day as me. To my astonishment, he walked up to the window and collected his visa ... just like that.

My heart pounded as I stepped up to the counter. The man behind the glass looked up at me. He motioned for me to wait while he placed a phone call. He walked to the back room to check the fax machine. Returning to his desk, he sorted through the stack of passports to find my documents – the same stack he sorted through for the Taiwanese man.

This could be it, I thought. *Don't get too excited, Jeremy, but it looks like you've got your visa.*

When he found my passport, the official flipped it open to a fresh page and then, sliding it under the glass he said, "There is no visa code for you here. It might come in a few minutes. Please sit down."

From a chair in the waiting room, I watched as Australian, Taiwanese, French, Japanese, and Estonian travellers all walked away with smiling faces. As it approached closing time for visa services, I had yet to see a happy Canadian. The time had come for security to lock the heavy wooden doors. Still I waited. I clung to a shred of hope to the very end, but I knew.

At last I checked with the official one more time. He made a phone call. He checked the fax machine, but returned shaking his head. He clasped his hands as if in prayer and said, "If it comes in on Tuesday, I'm at your service." I smiled at him and nodded.

Storming back to the hostel, I decided to abandon all hope of reaching Iran. I retired early that night, weary and uncertain of my next move. My plans for this trip had fallen apart. I knew I had to ride in the morning, but as I switched off the lights, I still had no idea where.

CHAPTER 11

I stopped at a gas station on the way out of town to put air in the drive tire. It had a slow leak. I examined the wear bars. At least the tread looked all right. A passer-by noticed me fumbling with the long air chuck and came over to watch. When I propped the bike up to oil the chain, he asked where I was headed.

"Syria," I mumbled.

"Ah!" he said. He traced out the route on my map that I had taken once before to Ankara.

"No. I'll go here," I said. I pointed to a line that zigzagged like a crack in a concrete driveway all the way to Turkey's southern coast.

"No, no," he insisted. "Ankara all the way."

"Yes. I know it's the most efficient way, but it's boring." I could hear an edge in my voice. I took a slow breath and went on a little calmer, "I'm going here, to Antalya." I pointed again. The stranger nodded. Then he wished me well and walked away, waving to me as I rode towards the Galata Bridge.

My green motorcycle darted through traffic beneath a canopy of red flags, all hung in preparation for the upcoming national holiday. Banners with Turkey's white star and crescent moon hung from tall buildings, while smaller flags dangled from lines strung up between light posts.

Flags lit up everything from apartment windows to

bridges, but they failed to brighten the sky. Dark and overcast, the heavens foreshadowed a storm. Everything remained dry for the moment, but I wore my rain gear anyway.

Making sure to pay all the tolls this time, I followed the same grey road that had brought me to Ankara a week earlier, only this time I was on my way to Syria. I remembered riding that day beneath a McDonald's spanning the road like a bridge. I had scoffed at it then, but this time it drew me in. When we fall, we fall hard.

I walked inside carrying my helmet. It took a lot of effort to move my boots up those stairs. Everything on the menu looked the same as I stood in line to order. I sat down on a plastic chair at a plastic table and sucked Coke through a plastic straw. The building shook as large trucks passed beneath and I sat there, looking down at the highway.

Why did I feel so deflated? Why could I not get excited about new possibilities? It's not like I had chosen Iran with a great deal of care. In fact, I'm not even sure that I chose it at all. Thinking back, I just sort of found myself on that path after I told a friend that I might go. A flippant statement gathered momentum, became a legitimate resolution, and carried me along like a cork on a river towards the completion of an ill-conceived goal. I would ride to Iran. It seemed like a reasonable idea, but once I had Iran on the brain, I stumbled on as if it were the *only* destination, as if I had found the *only* path. What a stupid way to make a major decision.

Another large truck approached. It rumbled out of view below the building and I could feel the vibration. Shifting to look at my reflection in the glass, I saw a troubled expression. It had just occurred to me how one could draw a parallel between how I had chosen Iran and how I had chosen my religion.

Maybe Chikako was right to ask about beliefs based on

nationality. After all, I grew up in the West, was born into a faith, plopped onto a path and pointed in a direction before I could examine anything objectively. If my life had begun in the Middle East, I'd probably be a Muslim. Hell, I had chosen my motorcycle with greater care than I had chosen my God. And look at how well that turned out.

My motorcycle ... I looked down at it in the parking lot. *Shit!* The headlight was on. That meant I had also left the key in the ignition. Was I so upset about choosing another destination that I hoped to sabotage the entire trip?

Jumping to my feet, I stuffed a large amount of greasy paper and plastic in the trash and hurried back to the machine. It was a welcome distraction, actually. I didn't have the energy or desire to start thinking about the validity of my belief system. I find it draining. I suspect it drains everyone. Maybe that's where dogma comes from. People piece together a world view when they're young and then spend the rest of their lives defending it because they're tired.

I wondered why, after so many years of coasting, I had started to think about God again. Was it the adhan from the Blue Mosque? The conversation with Chikako? Or did the McDonald's remind me of church? No. This time it probably had something to do with my location. Riding through the Middle East without considering God, I thought, is like sailing the around the world ignoring the ocean.

After checking the neutral indicator light, I pushed the starter button. I let it idle while I made some adjustments to my riding gear. Finally I brushed my hair back with my hand and pulled on the helmet.

Rolling again, I turned away from the highway to ride south into the mountains. It had warmed up enough that I could ride with an open visor. With the sun beaming on my face and my rain gear neatly packed away, I calmed myself with clichés to the effect of "the journey is the destination," and so forth. The very same platitudes that would have irritated me moments earlier buoyed my spirits now as I rode through steep mountains covered with dense greenery.

Though I tried not to fixate on the thought for fear of ruining a perfectly good ride, I wondered if these same mottos had any spiritual application. Is searching for God more important than finding God? I couldn't imagine a cleric within the big three monotheistic religions nodding his head to that question, but what about the laity?

C.S. Lewis, one of Christianity's most beloved writers, may have at least given it thoughtful consideration. In the final book of *The Chronicles of Narnia*, Lewis introduces a character who spends his entire life serving a false god, but ends up sharing the same reward as those who followed the one true God. On the merit of his (albeit misguided) faith, he essentially walks through the door to the wrong afterlife.

In *The Screwtape Letters*, Lewis observes that we would do better praying to God as he knows himself to be, rather than to the God we think we know. This well-respected Oxford don acknowledged gaps in his understanding of God, and even the probable existence of significant flaws.

Of course he did. If God created us, then he is more complex than we are. Lewis understood that. Honestly, I often fail to understand the workings of my own mind, let alone those of another person. How could I claim to know *God*?

The more I think about God, the less I claim to know. At best, I struggle to believe. Usually I just hope, and even that gets hard.

As I came around a bend, the landscape opened up into a broad valley with orchards and olive groves. Summer kept a firm toehold in this part of the world. Only certain fruit trees and the harbingers of winter themselves, the poplars, showed any sign of fall colour. The Oscillator carried me into the warm wind and I smiled.

"I can explore other possibilities," I told myself. "I can let go of Iran. After all, roads are for journeys, not destinations."

CHAPTER 12

After spending just four hours in the saddle, I decided to stop for the day. I had gotten a late start anyway, and it looked as if the sun wouldn't hang about much longer. The main road pushed through blocky buildings in an anonymous town and I parked the bike off to the side.

Before I could remove my helmet, an old man in a leather jacket approached. A smouldering cigarette exercised squatter's rights in one of several vacant lots between his yellow teeth. His weathered face had character all right, but if I had to single out his most distinguishing characteristic, I'd say it was probably the yawning black hole at the base of his throat. Yeah. The yawning black hole.

The man seemed to have an urgent message, but as he spoke no English, or for that matter had no larynx with which to vocalize language, it was hard to decipher. While I stared at the neck-hole, he produced an array of clicks, whistles, and farting noises that sounded like R2-D2 calling a cat.

I think he scolded me for parking on his turf, but when I pointed to the Canadian flag on my bike I heard a softer edge in his sound effects. He tapped his chest and said, "*Click-[motorboat sound]-phtttth.*" I took this to be his name.

Click grabbed my arm and pulled me towards a hotel. And that's how I ended up in the back room of a furniture store surrounded by tough men in suits.

It happened that fast. I didn't like the looks of these guys, nor the way that one of them stood directly behind my chair at all times. Click sat beside me, tooting away in the direction of a large man behind a heavy wooden desk. The table lamp had a metal shade that reflected glaring light at me while casting a thick shadow on him. His dark form nodded through a swirling cloud of cigarette smoke as my guide gurgled on.

When the man snapped his fingers, one of his cronies placed a cup of tea in my hand. A cartoon bubble of Smiley from the Canadian Embassy appeared in my head: "Whatever you do, if someone offers you a drink, don't accept it. People have been drugged and robbed."

I had laughed him off then, but I wasn't laughing now. Looking around the room, this seemed like a den of thieves. Lifting the cup to my lips, I blew over the surface to help it cool, and also to check people's reactions. My eyes darted about. Had anyone noticed my apprehension? I pretended to take a sip. I'm so clever. How about now? Were they watching me?

No one seemed to notice that I hadn't touched my drink. After a few more pretend sips, I chuckled at my silly paranoia. Then, raising my glass to Click, I took an actual drink. Everyone turned to look at me. *Oh crap.*

But they only did so because they had thought of the perfect hotel. The man behind the desk stood up, much less menacing now that I could see him. He drew me a map for a hotel and sent me away – after I finished my tea.

With the Oscillator locked up on the sidewalk in front of the hotel, I took the stairs up to my room. Sitting on the edge of the bed, I reached into a black plastic bag to remove a can of Efes tightly wrapped in newspaper. They wrap the cans in paper so that people can't tell that you're drinking beer, I guess. It also keeps the cans nice and cool. I removed the paper slowly, tossing it on the floor.

Mahmoud had e-mailed again. He claimed that his confusion over the fax fiasco rivalled my anger. He promised to have an answer for me in the morning, but I knew for a fact that his office was closed for the next two days. More lies.

Smoke permeated the fabric in this room, too. My eyes watered. When they closed, I slipped into a nightmare.

Lost in the warren of a vast bazaar, I could feel the presence of a companion. I never saw him, but I knew it was my younger brother. You sense these things in dreams. We lingered, my brother and I, pushing through the merchant city, unaware of the growing darkness.

In front of us the market was still busy. There were men in turbans bartering over spices, women in chadors fingering bolts of cloth, and children pawing at carts brimming with sticky sweets. Behind us I could hear the rumble of overhead metal doors as they unspooled, banging shut against the stone threshold of every shop. I turned to face a black and desolate lane. As I did, the sound of rolling doors echoed at my back. Spinning again, I caught a glimpse of a solitary merchant. He looked at me. Then he extinguished the last electric light before vanishing.

My brother and I quickened our pace, our shoes scuffing over wet cobblestones in the dark. He followed close behind as I hurried along, eyes straining for a source of light to lead us home. The darkness veiled something sinister.

Turning from the main corridor, we ducked into a narrow alley, but heavy Persian carpets hung from overhead lines, blocking our path. An unforgiving presence followed, but now it followed only me. I was alone. Frantic, I pushed through the rugs, driving into them with heavy legs and clawing my way through the alley, running, running, running.

Then I awoke. I was lying on my side, facing the window, and it took my eyes a moment to adjust to the dim light. It took my mind another few seconds to orient itself.

Where am I?

I exhaled. *Just a dream. Nothing to fear.* I closed my eyes. *Just a dream.*

I remained still as a stone, on my side, taking shallow breaths. Someone was in the room.

No. You had a nightmare. You're alone. Nothing to fear.

But someone *was* there, in the dark. I could feel it. Perhaps that's what stirred me awake – a quiet footfall, or the creak of a door. Now the stranger sensed that he had disturbed me, and he stood very still, hoping that I would just go back to sleep.

I had to squeeze my eyelids to keep them shut. When I relaxed the pressure just a bit, they sprang open.

I looked straight ahead to the window. No one there.

Of course not. You're being silly.

I raised my head up off the pillow, sweeping the room from left to right with my gaze.

See? Nothing to fear.

I propped myself up on an elbow. I turned my head to peer into the remaining shadows. There, at my shoulder, stood the very real form of a hulking man dressed in black.

He stood against the edge of my bed, so menacing. The shock of him standing there hit me like ice water. My heart pounded – one time – harder than I ever thought it could. It felt like I had been punched in the chest from the inside.

I never cried out. Instead, with all the strength that fear provides, I reared up to fight. The man didn't flinch. He just stood there, watching.

I squinted at him through the dark, trying to understand. Was he wearing my motorcycle jacket and rain gear? No, actually, it *was* my motorcycle jacket and rain gear, which I had hung beside my bed. I reached out and touched it to be sure before lying back down, my heart still beating hard and fast. I fixed my eyes on the jacket for some time, half expecting it to move. At this point in a horror movie, that's exactly what would happen. Finally I closed my eyes.

For the next hour I lay awake in bed, no longer afraid, just unable to rest. I could do nothing to quiet my thoughts but whisper my mantra, *I'm sorry. I'm sorry. I'm sorry.*

Exactly when this became a habit, I can't remember ... probably when I was a teenager. I do it less now that I'm older, but sometimes I still apologize in the night. It calms me.

I'm sorry.

I never apologize for anything in particular. I don't even apologize to anyone in particular. I only know that I *am* sorry. About that, at least, I'm sincere.

I'm sorry.

Over and over. I count contritions like other people count sheep. In Hemingway's *A Farewell to Arms,* a character talks to a priest about God: "I'm afraid of him in the night, sometimes," he says.

So am I.

I'm sorry

CHAPTER 13

Spreading the map out the next morning, I identified the anonymous town as Bozüyük. I refolded the map, sliding it into the plastic window on my tank bag so I could see the day's ride. As it normally carried all my cold-weather gear, the bag became a floppy map holder on days like this, when I wore every layer.

I planned a short ride but soon got caught up in the momentum, neglecting to stop even for food. When fatigue caught up with me, I walked into the ditch and collapsed on a hummock of gravel. I slept there, still wearing my helmet, until a concerned motorist stopped to check on me.

A farmer worked his field with a rusty open-cab tractor as I rolled south through the prairies. Coming over a rise, I caught my first glimpse of the Mediterranean. It stretched out to the horizon, shimmering silvery-grey in the dull light like a buttered cookie sheet. As I rode closer, the water darkened into shades of blue and green marbled with white foam. Vendors dotted the highway along the coast, roasting corn on wood fires.

In the seaside town of Antalya, I found a hotel with a cool green courtyard wreathed in pink flowers where I could work on my bike. But first I drank a beer and fell asleep for thirteen hours.

At Anamur, the road entered a swath of charred forest. The

smoke had cleared, but the smell of burnt timber remained, mingling with the scent of fresh sawdust. Men walked along the steep slopes through blackened trees, cutting logs with simple tools and dragging them out with horses. Colour returned to the forest after a few kilometres, along with the fragrance of pine needles. It felt good to ride in the shade. Climbing into the hills and then dropping back to the coast, the road played with the sea like a child at the beach.

The sound of waves splashing against round stones on the shore greeted me as I pulled into the gravel lot of a seaside restaurant. I took a seat on the patio and squinted out at the sparkling water. A chubby man with a moustache and white apron clasped his hands with joy when he saw me, but we couldn't communicate with each other. He took me to the back kitchen where he pointed at different meats in the fridge. Each time, I imitated the sound I thought the animal would make if it were alive, and he clapped with pleasure. Finally, to order, I just bleated like a lamb.

The waiter brought out peppers and strips of lamb sizzling on a cast-iron plate. I guzzled two bottles of Coke, and the owner brought me a free chai when I had finished the meal.

I sipped my tea in the sunshine and listened to the water. I needed to take more breaks on this trip. And the Oscillator could use a rest as well.

In addition to the constant wobble in the front end, that day I noticed a new symptom. There was a disturbing *clunk* whenever I hit a bump or applied the brakes with any force. The sound seemed to originate from beneath my instrument cluster, which might indicate a faulty steering head bearing, but Quy would have caught that. I thought back to those frantic days in his garage. Yes, he had repacked those bearings. The damage must be in the forks.

By this time, I had adapted my riding style to the wobble in the forks. Repacking the gear had helped, but I also rode smoother in turns. If I held the bars steady through the curves it felt all right, but I knew that if I had to make a quick adjustment, say, in an emergency, I would crash.

The hour was late when I reached Mersin, but I felt strong. Finding accommodation shouldn't be a problem, I thought, as I had passed dozens of hotels over the last hundred kilometres, so I decided to press on.

If I had taken a closer look at my map, I might have reconsidered. Because after Mersin, the road abandoned the coast with its quaint tourist hotels and ploughed into a dirty shipping hub clogged with transport trucks. Over an hour passed without sighting a single hotel, let alone an acceptable one.

Cities ran together to form one grey mass of blocks, making it impossible to pinpoint my location. Not that I could risk a glance at my map. As the day's final call to prayer penetrated the smog, I hit a veritable stampede of traffic.

When I spotted refuge at last, I flung myself from the mayhem and landed, skidding to a halt, on the brick drive of "Le Grande Hotel," a grimy building that optimistically displayed two stars. I settled into my room well after dark. After a hot shower, I wrapped a towel around my waist and lay down on the bed.

Here, near the border with Syria, I needed a plan I needed two plans, really – one for my destination and another to fix the Oscillator. I stared at the ceiling.

If I took the bike apart myself, I might destroy it. Watching me tinker with machines is like watching a Charlie Chaplin film. Anyway, I didn't have the parts. That meant finding a Kawasaki dealer or, failing that, getting a friend in Canada to ship the parts to me … either way, a lengthy delay.

Where would I get my friends to ship the parts to, anyway? I didn't even know where I was exactly. The moment I rode away from Iran I got lost. I was lost all the time. Am I making good progress? Don't know. Am I halfway through my journey? Perhaps.

Oh, I intended to visit Syria, but then what? Jordan? Then what? I just needed some place to go.

The residual heat from my shower floated off my skin to lend what comfort it could to the drafty room. I could feel muscles tighten up. I rolled over onto my side and swung my legs off the bed, using the momentum to rock into a seated position. On my feet, I straightened up inch by inch, careful not to make sudden moves. Then I reached high, stretching my fingertips as far as they would go and looking past them to the ceiling. Removing my towel, I spread it on the floor. I knelt upon it, bending forward until my head touched the ground. If anyone could see me now they might think I was in prayer, except that I was naked. Actually, I've always felt naked while praying.

I held the stretch for a minute while my vertebrae clicked into place. Then I got back up and sat on the bed. We had so much in common, the Oscillator and I. We were both wounded and lost, just two vagabonds limping along trying to find our way.

CHAPTER 14

Before I could stop him, the bellboy polished my helmet with Pledge, leaving it lemony-fresh and real slippery. For the next several days it would pop out of my hands every time I grabbed it, but I could usually bobble it around so it never hit the floor. Waving goodbye, I took a deep breath of lemon-scented air and timed my departure to hit a slim break in traffic.

Hours later, heading east out in the country, I stopped at a mechanics shop with dozens of old tires piled on the roof. I had lost my stem puller in Croatia, and I thought that tightening the valve in my drive tire might stop the leak.

A chubby man with dark hair and a grey T-shirt frowned at me from the shadow of his doorway. Hoping to break the ice, I smiled and reached out to shake his hand.

"Do you speak English?" I asked.

"Fifty-fifty," he said. Then he giggled like a little girl on a Shetland pony. His name was Ebo, and if he honestly believed his English was "fifty-fifty," then he's got no idea how many words we have. In fact, even though he had memorized a few English phrases, questions mostly, he couldn't deal with the answers.

"Where you from?" he asked, meaning, "Where are you from?"

"Canada," I said, pointing to the flag on my bike. Ebo nodded.

"Where you from?" he asked again, meaning, "Where are you going?"

"Syria," I said, but he didn't understand.

"What time?" asked Ebo, pointing to my watch. I showed him. "Tea time!" he announced.

Ebo ushered me into a dim office and walked around to sit behind his metal desk. The cool air smelled earthy, with a subtle hint of lemon still wafting off my helmet. Apart from that it smelled of gear oil and rubber, just like my grandfather's old barn. There were oil stains on the concrete floor. An abandoned swallow's nest clung to the ceiling in the corner above a grey bed with rumpled blankets. A few canisters of solvent and motor oil sat collecting dust on a shelf beneath dirty windows, while a small coffee table and two plastic chairs rounded out the furniture.

I sat down with two other men, presumably Ebo's employees, though a clear link was never established. Duan was of average everything – medium height, medium build, middle-aged – while Ünal was wrinkled, tall, and slender, with a thick grey moustache and a beige suit. Ünal put the kettle on. Then he strapped a large plastic jug to his bicycle and pedalled down the highway to get more water. In the meantime, I smoothed my map out on Ebo's desk, showing him the route I had taken from Germany.

Ünal returned by the time the one-burner stove had heated up the water, and we had our tea. The cartoon bubble containing Smiley and his warning appeared fuzzy in my mind, but I did scan the faces of everyone in the room for signs of malice. With these guys I never bothered taking a pretend sip.

The men came out to see me off. Ebo handed me the supplies I needed, but he refused payment. I watched the three of them in my mirror, waving and growing smaller as I rode away.

The road dodged eastward around hills evenly spread with round trees and light-coloured rock. I paused at a high point overlooking a vast floodplain. In the distance I could see the superhighway, straight and fast, raised in its arrogance on concrete pillars. That was the road I had been on, but I was happier now that I had found a less efficient secondary road, one that meandered to explore new things.

The Oscillator and I continued through fields of trees in furrowed red earth, past stone walls and the ruins of an ancient castle that looked down on us from above. A family worked together, spreading white blankets on the ground to catch olives that they stripped from a tree.

I had already passed the three most logical crossings into Syria, yet I continued riding east, roughly following the border. The thought of riding into Northern Iraq, what many people referred to as Kurdistan, appealed to me, but I knew that the crossing would be closed – the Turks had an active military campaign in the region to flush out the PKK. I had seen military convoys heading that way.

I rolled into Nizip for the night with the intent of taking a run at the Syrian border in the morning. Failing to find a hotel right away, I stopped every hundred metres or so for directions until I found a young man who knew a place.

"We go together," he said. Before I knew what to say about that, he hopped on the bike. Squished together in the space between my gas tank and duffle bag, we rode to a cheap hotel where the man got off, tipped his hat and walked away.

Riding south from Birecik, I arrived at a sunny dot on the border. Leaving Turkey was easy. I rode between two armed guards, where I encountered a crowd that greeted me with shouts of, "Welcome to Syria!" They were all standing by their vehicles waiting to clear into Turkey.

However, I was not so optimistic. I was on Syrian soil, yes, but I had yet to clear Immigration. According to all the official websites, if Syria has an embassy in your home country, then that is where you must apply for your visa. Syria had an embassy in Canada. If for some reason a traveller needed a visa while on the road, then the applicant must call on the Syrian embassy of a neighbouring country. After getting the letter of introduction from Smiley, I never followed through with the Syrian embassy, because it was closed for the weekend and I had been called back to Istanbul to pick up my visa for Iran. Every official channel insisted that a person could not obtain a visa at the border. These guys might very well send me back to Ankara.

A few uniformed men sat beside a pool of murky water, drinking maté. One of them put his gourd down and motioned for me to hand over my passport. He gave it a cursory glance and said, "Welcome to Syria." He sent me riding through the water towards a police checkpoint where a friendly crowd of officers gathered. They pointed me towards Immigration after taking my carnet.

I sat in a cramped room with five men, all in uniform, all smoking, while they checked my papers. Stacks of drawers stuffed with file cards reached to the ceiling. As one man looked through my passport, another handed me a cigarette and gave me a light.

When they discovered that I had no visa, they patched me through via cell phone to an official in Damascus. His voice crackled on the line.

"You cannot cross here," he said. "You do not have a visa, and this crossing cannot issue one. You must go to Kilis."

"At Kilis," I said, "they can process me there?"

"Yes, I think so."

"Where is this crossing?" I asked. "Is it too late to try and cross today?"

"Kilis is about one hundred kilometres to the west. I think you should make it today."

The man wished me luck and hung up the phone.

Back I rode, through the water, past the crowd, between the armed guards and into Turkey. A Turkish police officer suggested a shortcut to Kilis, and I took off.

A country lane cut through a parched land and past shacks of mud and stone before bursting into green fields of corn and pomegranate trees. When the lane connected with a major road, I stopped for lunch at a gas station.

I pulled up at the border around one in the afternoon. This border station was much bigger than the last one. It processed buses and transport trucks. After a quick passport check, a big iron gate rolled aside and I motored through. There was a crowd here, too, but it didn't shout, "Welcome to Syria!"

A guard snatched the passport from my hand.

"Where are you going?" he demanded.

"Damascus."

"Then where? Jordan?"

"Yes."

He looked me straight in the eyes. "Then Israel?" he said.

"No. Of course not."

"Good."

I slid my passport through the glass to the man on the other side. When he realized that I had no visa, he called to a stocky man with a moustache who ushered me into the back. Now we were all on the same side of the glass. He seated me at a desk and walked away. Men in uniform sat with their backs to me, typing away on computers stained grey by the smoke from thousands of cigarettes. Through the window, I watched travellers handing their papers over to be stamped.

The stocky man returned with his superior, who took a stern tone. It might have intimidated me, but whenever tension mounted the stocky man would sabotage his commander by cracking a joke. He even offered me a cigarette at one point, as if to a man before a firing squad. Everyone laughed, including the commander.

With the questioning over, the officer faxed my papers to Damascus and told me to wait. In the meantime, the stocky man took me to the bank, where I paid for my visa. When Damascus faxed back my application, he smiled and put a fleet of postage stamps into my passport. He pounded them with a rubber stamp and let me go.

After a few more trips to the bank to pay various fees, the gate to Syria rolled open. I looked down at the map of Turkey on my tank bag. There looked to be a major road running south from my location but, before I could see where it went, the page ended. I frowned. The Oscillator and I were about to ride off the map.

CHAPTER 15

The first twenty kilometres inside any country – that's the best ride. Your rear fender points and laughs at bureaucracy while the front fender aims at new things. Riding without a guidebook or map makes the tremors of excitement even more jarring. It's hard to hold the bike steady. But when one reaches the dizzying traffic of a major city and has no map, then the taste of freedom quickly sours. What city is this, anyway?

When the traffic bogged down, I yo-yoed past the same car for several blocks. Every time I passed the man he looked over, grinning. He shot his arm out the window with a big thumbs-up, and I lifted my visor when we stopped side by side.

"Hotel?" I said.

Wide-eyed, the driver nodded so enthusiastically that his face went blurry. We progressed together in a series of lurches past a monochrome city of cinderblock apartments and boxy buildings, all adorned with dusty air-conditioning units and window shutters. Now crawling along, we arrived at a square in the heart of Aleppo ringed with impatient, honking cars. The driver pointed at the hotel as he idled past. I waved thanks as I backed the bike up to the curb, and watched him inch away.

With its marble floor and bubbling fountain in the lobby,

I knew that this place would not suit my budget. They wanted forty dollars a night. I looked out at the traffic, then back at the concierge.

"Um," I mumbled, avoiding eye contact, "do you know of another place nearby? A cheaper place?" He did not.

Back outside in the long shadows of late afternoon, I surveyed the river of traffic. It was now clogged with a flotilla of yellow taxis like so many rubber ducks at the Lumsden Duck Derby. To get anywhere in this mess required a plan. I could walk, but I hated to leave the Oscillator unguarded on the street. What I didn't know at the time is that I could have left the bike there without a care in the world. Syria has always faced many problems, but petty theft is not one of them.

There was an old man nearby roasting peanuts on the back of his bicycle. He had a black wood-burning stove with a long, slender stovepipe behind the seat, and the peanuts roasted on a metal pan on top. I bought a bag and sat down next to my bike to think.

As I considered my options, two young men approached. Hussein, with his blue-grey eyes and fair complexion, had an eastern European look about him. He had wavy brown hair and a dull sweater with the word "FOLD" emblazoned on the chest. He spoke almost no English, which made him appear rather shy.

His friend, Mahmoud, on the other hand, embraced me. He fawned over me like a long-lost brother, exclaiming, "Welcome! Welcome!" He did this with such alarming frequency that I feared I might need to slap him. Mahmoud had a more conventional appearance for this part of the world, tan skin and brown eyes. He had the makings of a dark beard if he would let it grow, and he wore a pair of stylish glasses. A red golf shirt hung loosely from his slender frame.

When they learned I needed a place to stay, they offered

to help. Taking me by the arm, Mahmoud led me to a nearby hotel. The corner balconies on the white building were rounded and draped with strings of white lights. It had blue neon signs on the roof and running vertically down the side that read, "Ramsis Hotel." It was cheaper than the first place, but still kind of expensive. Coming out of the Ramsis, I spotted a dark building across the street with a small, plain hotel sign that charged twenty dollars per night – probably the best I could do this late in the day in that part of the city. I booked in immediately.

My two new friends insisted that I join them for supper. I couldn't refuse, they said. I did, however, need a moment to change and a little time alone. When Mahmoud realized the implications of this – that we would be parted momentarily – his face grew sombre. He trudged out of the room to wait for me in the lobby. His spirits quickly recovered, though, and the last thing I saw disappearing behind the closing door was Mahmoud's beaming smile.

"Welcome!" he said.

Removing my armoured motorcycle jacket and pants felt like taking off steel-toed boots at the end of a long workday. The pants, with their padded knees and zippered vents, provided comfort enough for riding, but they inhibited my natural stride when I walked and the material scratched against my legs. I rolled them up and threw them on the bed beside my helmet.

With cupped hands, I splashed cool water on my face. I wet my tangled hair and smoothed it back. I washed my hands and arms up to the elbows. Then I dried off and sat down on the narrow bed to take a long drink from my water bottle. Knowing that I would fall asleep if I lingered for too long, I stood up and stretched as high as I could. Then I got dressed.

Though the sun had set, the night was still warm. I buttoned up a short-sleeved shirt and pulled on beige cargo pants. Compared to my riding gear, these clothes felt like silk pyjamas. I tapped my leg below the knee to verify that I had my leg wallet with all my important papers. Then I dropped a camera in the side pocket of my pants before returning to the bathroom to splash more water on my face.

After leaving my room, I found Mahmoud chatting with two old men. The pair must have owned the building, because they sat in cushy chairs in the lobby beneath a photograph of themselves in cushy chairs in the lobby. I wanted to check the photo to see if it had another picture of them in the background, but there was no time. When Mahmoud spotted me, he jumped to attention.

The three of us went out for burgers and fries. As we walked, Mahmoud kept reaching for my hand, holding it with interlocking fingers. Or he tried to link arms with me. It's just part of the culture, I know that. But I had just met this guy and, well, I'm just not that affectionate.

Mahmoud blocked cars for me when we crossed the street. He motioned for people to stand aside. He coddled me. Whenever Mahmoud released my arm for a moment, I repositioned it to make it difficult for him to grab again, but he always managed somehow. When I finally lifted my hands in the air like I was under arrest, I think he got the message. After that, he still reached for my arm, but it happened less frequently.

When our food came, Mahmoud and Hussein got into a minor slapping fight over who got the honour of paying. We took everything to go, and ate on the edge of park that had been piled with garbage. Afterwards, we tossed our own rubbish over our shoulders. Then Mahmoud and Hussein brought me to meet another friend, still hard at work in his office long after dark. A middle-aged man, well-dressed with light skin, Afram spoke fluent English.

He stopped what he was doing to prepare tea for us all, with mint leaves floating in the cups. After that, Mahmoud and Hussein stood to leave, effectively transferring charge of my well-being to Afram. Mahmoud took me by the shoulders and kissed me on both cheeks. Then, smiling, he said, "Welcome," and walked out the door.

If it seemed strange to Afram that he suddenly had to take care of a foreigner, he never let on. He tidied up a few things at work and showed me out to his car, as if this sort of thing happened all the time.

"What do you plan on seeing here in Aleppo?" he asked me.

"I don't know. Actually, I hadn't thought about it. I don't really know anything about the city."

"You don't know anything about Aleppo?" said Afram. "We'll go to your hotel, but first I want to show you the citadel. It's quite famous. Aleppo is one of the oldest cities in the world, you know."

"I didn't know that."

Afram said that Aleppo has a history that stretches back around eight thousand years. Just a short ride to the south, Damascus claims to be one of the world's oldest capitals.

During my time with Mahmoud and Hussein, I had seen a few women walking around, but they always seemed to have male chaperones. They wore conservative clothing, certainly headscarves, but many also wore long black chadors. As darkness fell, even these conservatively dressed women disappeared until there were only men out on the streets. Now Afram drove me through a part of the city where there were still many women out on the town, and they weren't even wearing anything to cover their heads. It was a warm night. Men and women sat at a restaurant patio, mixing freely, and if I wasn't mistaken, there was beer on the table in front of them.

"This is the Christian part of the city," explained Afram. Just like in other Middle Eastern cities, if a traveller wants to find a drink in Aleppo, he or she must first find the Christians.

Afram stopped the car at an intersection. In North America, we look past the junction to traffic lights on the other side, but Syrian traffic lights are on the near corner where our stop lines would be. In theory, this should force drivers to stay back in order to see the light, but it only works that way in Europe. In the Middle East, the first row of cars stops right at the intersection, ahead of the signal. They wait there until motorists lined up behind them – motorists who can see the light – start honking when it goes green.

"Why do they do that?" I asked.

Afram shook his head, "I don't know," he sighed. "It always causes a delay. First the light changes, then the cars honk. Then the cars in front react to the honking. Then they move. It's stupid."

The light turned green and Afram laid on the horn to get the traffic moving.

"So stupid," he said.

Soon the citadel of Aleppo came into view at the apex of a conical hill. Floodlights shone against weathered limestone, making the castle glow like a halo on a black-light cherub. A dusty moat encircled the base of the round hill and we walked the perimeter, following a broad path of smooth paving stones. We stopped to survey the entrance, a black arch in a formidable barbican at the base of the hill. A stone path on thick pillars spanned the moat between the tower and another imposing arch high above in the castle wall.

"This is the most famous castle in Aleppo," Afram said.

Indeed. It's the kind of castle that tourists like me seek out when they travel. Every single person who visits Aleppo sees it. They have to. The guidebook commands us. I usually feel blasé about such attractions but, having arrived without a guidebook, I felt a sense of amazement – like I had discovered it for myself. No guidebook told me to come here. An actual resident of Aleppo took me, and that made a difference somehow.

We sat down on a bench and Afram pointed out a few landmarks.

"There's a good hammam. And if you go through that gate over there, that's a big bazaar. You should see it."

I had intended to move on in the morning, but Afram convinced me to stay a few more nights.

"Over there is the Hall of Justice. But," he said, lowering his voice and taking a quick look about, "there is no justice here. If you pay, you go free."

I must have raised an eyebrow or something, and Afram noticed.

"OK," he continued, "not if you kill something, or drugs or selling weapons or so. But all other things."

Safely inside his car on the way back to the hotel, Afram picked up the conversation where he had left off.

"People are afraid here," he said. "If I say something bad about the officials, in five minutes I'm in jail and no trace."

"You can't speak freely to anyone?" I asked.

"Well, perhaps to friends, quietly, that you trust. But to strangers, no. You cannot just say what you want. They might report you."

I wondered why he would tell me all this, but before I could ask he dropped me at the hotel.

It was, for me, the first foreshadowing of the unrest that

would eventually threaten to tear Syria apart during the so-called Arab Spring. Although there are exceptions to every rule I could guess from Afram's dissent that he was Sunni, a group that comprises the majority of Syrians and Muslims in general. If he were a Christian he would probably support the regime, not because they share an ideology with the ruling Alawites – also a minority group – but because the Alawites, and the Assad family in particular, have for decades kept everything in check. The methods they use (ubiquitous informants, fear, and brutal torture) may not please anyone, but they have been up until recently very effective at enforcing a kind of stability. In 1982, Hafez al-Assad, Bashar al-Assad's father, levelled the city of Hama to crush a Sunni rebellion. He killed thousands of people.

Later on the trip, I would meet Syrian exiles scattered throughout neighbouring countries, but especially in Lebanon. That's where I met Ahed Al Hendi.

Just a year before I met him, he had been arrested for criticizing the Syrian regime on a blog. Along with his cousin, Ahed was taken from a Damascus Internet café after the owner reported them to the Syrian secret police.

Stripped of his clothes, Ahed was held in solitary confinement in a windowless cell. He wrote the date on the door with a sliver of soap: December 15. When guards said that he would remain there indefinitely, he wrote the year: 2006.

From that cell, Ahed could hear screaming as guards tortured his cousin for the names of political dissidents. Only he didn't think the screams came from his cousin – Ahed thought he was dead.

"I asked about my cousin when they took me out for questioning," Ahed told me. "They said he died. And I believed them."

During questioning, Ahed asked for his clothes back, and finally the guards agreed. "I was very lucky," he said.

In some ways he was. Unlike his cousin, he was never physically tortured while in custody, though he cannot explain why.

"Maybe I did a better job of playing dumb," he suggested. "Or, maybe they got everything they needed from my cousin. The torture they use … they can make you say anything."

Whatever the reason, Ahed escaped physical injury and, following a week in solitary confinement, he was transferred to a crowded cell. He and his cousin were released after just one month in prison. In the weeks that followed, authorities often pulled Ahed in for questioning. Realizing that his life would never be the same in Syria, he fled to Jordan, Egypt, and Lebanon, where I eventually met him in Beirut.

Outraged by what he had endured, and finally able to speak freely away from his home country he said, "Last Christmas I was in prison. This Christmas I am in exile. I wonder what Santa will bring me next year." He paused to put out his cigarette. "Change. I hope for change."

Ahed got his wish, at least on a personal level. Eventually he emigrated to the United States, where he earned a degree in political science at the University of Maryland. He now lives in Washington, D.C., where he works as a contributor for CyberDissidents.org, a group dedicated to free speech for political bloggers.

His wish for change in Syria would not come in the form he wanted, and not until February 2011, when several school children were arrested in Daraa and tortured for scrawling anti-regime graffiti on a school. The kids were probably inspired by the wave of protests and revolutions that had begun in Tunisia in December 2010.

The mistreatment of these kids sparked protests in the

small southern town, protests that eventually spread across the nation in spite of violent crackdowns by the military. At the time of writing, it is estimated that the regime has been responsible for over thirty thousand deaths, and Syria is now engaged in a lopsided civil war.

Of course, I was ignorant about the political climate at the time, and I couldn't have foreseen any of this while on my motorcycle trip. But after speaking with Afram, and later with Ahed, I listened a bit more to what people were saying, and I noticed what they were not saying. From then on, the posters of Bashar al-Assad that hung on nearly every wall took on a new meaning.

CHAPTER 16

In the morning, I paid seventy-five cents for a taxi to the citadel, where I bought a ticket and hiked up the steep bridge. When I stepped over a crisp line of shade into the tower, the temperature dropped as if I had entered a meat locker. It spiked again on the other side when I re-entered the intense sunlight.

The citadel, with its sharp limestone blocks and clean lines, appeared wonderfully preserved from the outside, but inside it had all the appeal of a stone quarry. I climbed the ramparts to a high tower to take in a view of the surroundings. The mid-morning sun bounced off the pale city from blocky apartment buildings and domed mosques. Aleppo is a city that makes you squint. A grouping of yellow taxis stood out against the beige cityscape with the defiance of desert flowers. The bright flow of cars curved through the intersection to avoid the swinging baton of a traffic cop with an olive-green uniform and white hat.

Looking down and to the right, I watched a flock of pigeons circle an apartment building. A man stood on the roof, turning to face the birds. He whistled and waved a red flag on the end of a long pole. These men are called fanciers, and they play a forbidden game called *kash hamam* with the birds. The object of the game is to use your flock to lure away birds from other fanciers, thereby increasing the size of your flock.

I studied him for a long time, trying to figure out what he wanted the pigeons to do. I looked back at the traffic cop. I couldn't figure out what he wanted the cars to do, either.

Leaving the citadel, I entered the bazaar through the gate Afram had pointed out the night before. For a moment I was blind as my eyes fluttered to adjust to the shade. The hoofbeats of a donkey echoed off stone walls beneath a corrugated steel roof. I heard the smack of a stick against the animal's hide and sandals as they scuffed along the stone path, slapping at bare heels.

When I could see properly, I noticed that nearly a third of all men wore grey or black *didashahs*, a kind of robe like an ordinary dress shirt that extends down to the ankle. A few also wore suit jackets or vests and, if they wore a kafiya, it was red and white, always tied loosely, which allowed it to fall about their necks and shoulders. Many of them circled a string of prayer beads through their hand as they walked. The rest of the male population would have blended into any business-casual office in North America, except perhaps for their moustaches.

The women dressed in loosely fitted black robes, and they nearly always wore headscarves. A small number of them took modesty to the highest level, covering even their hands and faces so that one could detect no part of the individual. Seeing a woman dressed this way, my brain struggled to connect the image with a person. She reflected no light. Rather than seeing a woman in the market I saw darkness, like someone had punched a human-sized hole into a movie screen.

The use of veils has come to represent oppression of women to us in the West, but that was never the intention in the Muslim world. In fact, in *After the Prophet*, Lesley Hazleton explains that it was just the opposite:

In due course, another Quranic revelation dictated that from now on, [Muhammad's] wives were to be protected by a thin muslin curtain from the prying eyes of any men not their kin. And since curtains could work only indoors, they would soon shrink into a kind of minicurtain for outdoors: the veil.

The Revelation of the Curtain clearly applied only to the Prophet's wives, but this in itself gave the veil high status. Over the next few decades it would be adopted by women of the new Islamic aristocracy – and would eventually be enforced by Islamic fundamentalists convinced that it should apply to all women.

The souk was everything that had I wanted the Grand Bazaar in Istanbul to be: a crooked tunnel of chaos beneath vaulted stone ceilings, filled with bleeding donkeys and creaky wooden carts. There were shops piled with balls of honeyed pastry, while others displayed sheep heads, squiggly brains, and pink stomachs pressed flat against the glass. There were pyramids of coloured spices, walls of red rugs, bins of nuts, and a psychedelic mix of coloured turnip, pickles, peppers, and olives to look at, while the smell of roasted lamb and onion wrestled for attention against dust and dung. There were micro-vans about the size of overburdened donkeys, honking for people to squeeze up against the nearest wall so they could pass. Overhead, shafts of light poured in through breaks in the ceiling, momentarily spotlighting anyone who passed below.

As I pressed through the corridor taking it all in, I came upon a man struggling to secure a load onto a white donkey. Donkeys always look sad, but this one had just cause. Its face poked out from beneath tarps that concealed a cargo as tall and as broad as the beast itself. In an apparent attempt to outrun the burden, it lumbered forward before the man could cinch down the straps. In return, the man shouted at the beast, slapping and beating it.

I had already captured some good photographs of the scene when the man noticed me. He let go of the donkey to shout at me, shoving me back. This made for even better photographs, because the bundle began slipping off the donkey.

Noticing this, the man spun to attack the animal, which had already made some strides to extricate itself from the situation. At that moment, all three of us – the man, the donkey, and me – understood the implications for us all. If the man let go to shove me, the load would fall and the donkey would escape. A few shopkeepers figured that out as well, and they stood together, chuckling. I took more pictures, the man had his picture taken, and the sad donkey took its beating.

CHAPTER 17

In the morning, back at the hotel, I sorted through a bundle of maps. I would keep the large-scale one of Europe so I could point out my route to anyone who asked, but I would send the rest home. They were no good to me now. I picked up a free tourist map of Syria from the hotel lobby. That would do fine.

For this trip I had purchased two guidebooks. I hefted the one for Turkey onto my lap. Definitely send that home. It took up a lot of room and weighed more than my small camera. I put it down on the bed next to the pile of maps.

Turning next to the guidebook for Iran, I picked it up and held it, heavy in my hand. I leafed through the crisp, glossy pages, looking at pictures of mosques and mountains that I would never personally see. I sighed and took it out to the balcony, where I looked through it some more. It seemed ridiculous to carry this thing any farther, but I found it hard to let go. Finally I placed it on the "send home" pile, along with a pocket Farsi phrasebook. I'd buy an Arabic one if I could.

At the post office, a dynamic wad of humanity squished against the counter like a ball of Silly Putty pressed to a window. In this part of the Middle East, it seems like no one forms an orderly queue. Instead, everyone vies for attention by shoving forward until they come to within shouting distance of the attending service provider. It seems rude at first

– especially if you try to wait your turn – to have someone un-
abashedly squeeze past you to get served first, except that's
just how it works. You get used to it. Eventually I learned to
push with the best of them, gaining the pole position in seconds by muscling aside the weak and elderly. Actually, no, my
Canadian upbringing coupled with my Mennonite heritage
means that I come from penitent stock. I could never forgive
myself for shoving an old lady. Can you imagine? *Shove.* "Oh,
God, I'm so sorry." *Push.* "Forgive me, Lord!" No, I exhibited
restraint even while ploughing ahead.

I did, however, perform an experiment on one occasion.
Temporarily letting go of my inhibitions, I tried to see just
how pushy I could get without drawing ire from the people. I
used several techniques.

Crouching down, I snaked my hand through the crowd
and then, drawing my arm in like a horizontal bicep curl, I'd
drive my shoulder into the space it had created, neatly popping up in front of whoever stood before me. Given that I
stood a head taller than most in that group, I called this my
Whac-A-Mole method.

Although that was highly effective, I favoured a much
more entertaining approach. Standing as we all did, pressed
against the person in front of me, I'd move my face in nice
and close. When I could almost reach out with my tongue
to lick their ear, I'd say just softly, "Hello." As the person re-
coiled in shock, which they did invariably, I'd slip past them
in one smooth move while fixing upon them a crazy stare.
Genius.

Strangely enough, no matter how assertive I was, no
matter how rude, no one ever lost their temper. Not one time.

CHAPTER 18

The restaurant next to the hotel served a nice breakfast of olives, apricot spread, and thick slabs of soft white cheese with a basket of flatbread. The sweet smell of smoke from a narghile hung in the air, but not from my pipe. Instead I sipped some tea. In my mind I tried to work out how to repack the Oscillator so as to lower the centre of gravity and move the weight even farther forward, now that I had jettisoned some heavy guidebooks.

If I can just make a few more adjustments to the system, I thought, *maybe I can do without a repair shop until I find the perfect place for an extended stay.* In fact, it occurred to me that the roads here, with fewer mountains to negotiate, might even run straight. Unless the problem in my forks got worse, I could conceivably return to Canada and have the bike looked at then.

Before leaving the city, I needed fuel. There was a gas station within easy walking distance from my hotel, but easy walking and easy riding are two very different things. On foot I could cut across streets, walk counter to traffic flow, and spin around if I made a wrong turn at one of many indistinct landmarks, whereas on the bike I had to make snap decisions in thick traffic, traffic that would capitalize on the slightest error to sweep me off course. For this reason, I paced out my exact route. Actually, I walked it several times, noting landmarks, tricky intersections, and traffic flow on the narrow one-way streets. I had it dialled.

Straddling my bike, I threw a wave to the hotel doorman, who returned my gesture with a thumbs-up. Brimming with the confidence born of preparation, I rode fleet and true for thirty metres before banking into a hard right turn where I needed to go left. A yellow raft of taxis carried me downstream towards a strange quarter of the city, where the only thing I recognized was that familiar need to mitigate somehow the degree to which I had sabotaged my life.

Diving off the taxi-raft, it took me fifteen minutes of hectic riding to arrive at the hotel once again. The doorman gave me a thumbs-up.

I rode the correct route on round two and pulled into the station. Filling up the tank gave me a moment to review the directions the hotel clerk had given me. I wanted to ride east towards Deir ez-Zur for no other reason than how the roads looked on the tourist map. The one south of Aleppo appeared on the page as a thick purple line that cut straight through dozens of large towns, but the red line east looked thin and desolate, curving over the green paper along a blue Euphrates River. Also, to the east the map had a picture of a camel. With no guidebook, this seemed as valid a reason as any to choose a direction.

Paying the attendant, I hopped onto the bike, determined not to repeat the navigational errors that had wasted so much of my time already. Picking my way very carefully through the traffic now, it took me another fifteen minutes to end up right back at the very same gas station. I had certainly covered a lot of ground that morning, but I hadn't really gone anywhere – trapped in a *Family Circus* dotted-line comic. In fact, I had remained within a three-block radius of my hotel. I considered going back and checking in for another night, but I couldn't bear to face the doorman.

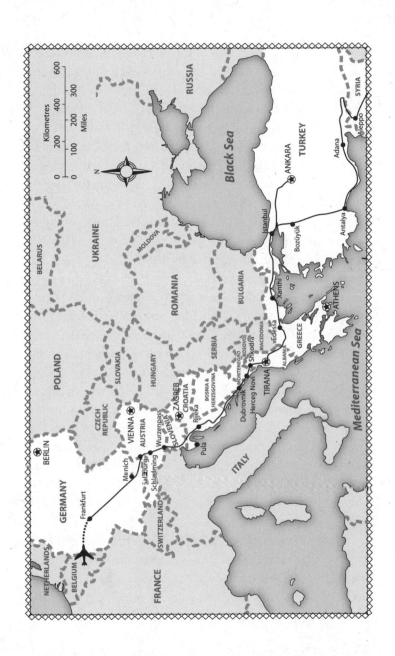

No, I soldiered on, and in the end I did find the correct road. Soon enough I arrived at the city's edge, riding past the living boundary stones of roadside vendors who perfumed the air with the rich scents of coffee and deep-fried falafel.

It was noon, and I was a mite peckish, but I failed to identify the right vendors in time to stop for a falafel. These guys sell food out of little trucks or stands by the road, but they specialize. Some serve only coffee. Others sell falafel. By the time I could see which one was which, I had sort of rolled past. Soon there were no more vendors and I just kept riding.

As the city diminished in my mirrors, the sound of a thousand honking cars yielded to that of rushing wind and the hum of my engine. I stood on the pegs to feel the clean air on my head and shoulders as I continued east. If I leaned forward while standing, stretching way out so that my head was over my front fender, I could just hear the wind. In this position, I could almost leave the motorcycle behind, as if I were flying, unencumbered and totally free.

Out here, the sky and the earth had fought to a stalemate, halving the frame of my visor into panels of blue and beige. Gone were the sharp buildings of chiselled stone from the city, replaced by rounded homes with mud plaster that bubbled up from the earth. Only a few dark clusters of square Bedouin tents and their flocks of sheep stood out vividly. Every other home appeared to be hiding beneath the folds of a brown blanket.

Golden kernels of corn had been spread into long rectangles alongside the road. Workers sifted through them, raking them, throwing them in the air with shovels, and sweeping at them to separate them from the chaff, before finally gathering them into piles for bagging.

As a little boy, maybe six or seven, I used to imagine that I had a sophisticated machine. The thing would render a perfect holographic image of a little boy, just like me, and I would control it remotely from a rolling sphere that made me invisible. I could stay there in my captain's chair while the hollow me interacted with my friends. It would say what I wanted and do what I wanted, or I could just let it go on autopilot and simply observe.

The hollow me would project a more confident image of myself, because it couldn't get embarrassed or shy. If the other kids teased it or didn't like it, that was fine. It wasn't me.

As I grew older, this theme of hiding carried on. I wanted, not a tree house, but an underground fort where no one could find me. I even built a frame out of hockey sticks once, and had started digging a hole to bury it in the backyard when my dad came home and put a stop to that.

And there were masks. I liked the silver Cobra Commander helmet that perfectly hid his face, and I wanted one. How cool, I thought, to be seen and hidden at the same time so that I could effectively live in my own private world inside that helmet, projecting an image of me that was not real.

That's how I feel when I put on a motorcycle helmet. I'm projecting an image and no one can see me. Not really.

That's what I was thinking as I slowed through the concrete and cinderblock town of Deir Hafer. I needed to find someplace to eat. When no clear option presented itself, I idled into a group of men milling about what appeared to be a filthy carnival but was in fact an outdoor market.

Not knowing what sort of reaction to expect, I switched off the bike and sat still on the dusty lot for a moment as I got my bearings. Judging by the way the crowd pressed in around me, I reasoned that Deir Hafer hadn't made the cut for the tourist bus itinerary. No scheduled stops here.

In these situations, surrounded by wide, unblinking eyes, I always move slow and deliberately. I wished I could keep my helmet on while moving through the crowd, but that would only draw more attention. Removing it, I hung it from the hook above my signal light while trying to appear as if I knew just exactly what I was doing. Whether or not it worked, I couldn't say, but the impression shattered the moment I began miming for food.

Most of the crowd, which had grown to about thirty people, started shouting, and a boy was dispatched to find an English guide. By the time I dismounted, the kid had returned with Bassam, a pudgy man in a striped golf shirt with a short goatee and dark hair. "Follow me," he said, and then, "It means 'Smiler.'"

"What? What does?" I asked, following close behind as we pushed through a wall of people.

"My name, Bassam. It means 'Smiler,' or..." – searching for the correct English phrase – "'... smiles a lot.'" He beamed as if to illustrate. He led me a short distance through the teeming market to a food stand with a big basin of boiling oil on a concrete floor. The place was so packed with people that it would have burst at the seams if it had had walls. He pushed through the men to place an order. Then he ushered me to the relative quiet of a space near the toilets. I plopped down on a red plastic chair to wait while Bassam hastened away to retrieve the food.

A soft tap on the elbow drew my attention to the kid who had originally found Bassam. He stretched out his hand, holding out for me the key to my motorcycle.

"Thanks," I said. For the all the care I take in unfamiliar situations, I have a nasty habit of leaving the key in the ignition. I stood up and walked a few paces to look out at my bike. Moustached men in *didashahs* and headscarves surrounded it, while dark-haired boys played with the signal lights and the zippers on my pack.

A boy in a greasy T-shirt, bent over the hot fryer, noticed my concern. From where he worked he had a clear view of the bike. He pointed to his eye and gave me a reassuring nod. I returned to my plastic chair.

Bassam returned with a falafel and a can of cold Pepsi. He sat with me while I ate, interpreting bits of conversation between me and several youths who he couldn't quite shoo away. He added suddenly, "Syrians love the peace!"

I nodded and waited for him to explain.

"We love Egypt, Saudi, Jordan, Turkey, Lebanon ... everyone!"

I nodded again, though I noticed a conspicuous absence on his list of countries. Here and there he dropped a soft hint that he disliked the policies of some western governments, but by his actions he said that he certainly had no problem with me.

When I stood to pay, Bassam said, "It is nothing, for free."

He saw me back to my bike along with a fresh swarm of people, young men, mostly. I hadn't seen a single woman all this time. As everyone looked on, I put in my earplugs and fastened my helmet.

"Safety first!" I shouted over the engine. Then I rode away, leaving the waving crowd behind.

Because of my late start, I gave up on reaching Deir ez-Zur before nightfall. It had been an arbitrary goal anyway. I rode over the Euphrates at Ar-Raqqah and found a cheap hotel that let me park the Oscillator in their foyer.

Later I joined the manager in the reception area for tea. Presumably for my benefit, he switched the television to an English-language cartoon called *The Happy Family*. The show revolved around a perpetually happy Muslim family that remained so because of their strict adherence to the laws of Islam. Along the way, *The Happy Family* intervened to correct the divergent behaviour of others. If you can believe it, this made them even happier. It was like watching *The Ned Flander's Show* without *The Simpsons.*

Several children rushed past me as I stepped outside. Shopkeepers were hosing down their floors and pushing the brown wastewater into the street with long-handled squeegees. Others flung water onto the road from a bucket to keep the dust down. Small 125-cc motorcycles, covered with carpet from gas tank to taillight, bounced along carrying two, three, or more helmetless passengers while weary horses stood by, hitched to garbage carts, oblivious to the honking of yellow taxis. The night air of Ar-Raqqah was never devoid of dust and cigarette smoke, but it was warm and pleasant.

I entered a teahouse, taking a seat beneath the ubiquitous posters of President Bashar al-Assad. I ordered a narghile.

This, I thought, *finally feels like the Middle East.* Though technically I had entered the region when I rode across the Bosporus in Turkey, it hadn't really felt like it until that moment. Even Aleppo, with all its novelty, still had a subtle European flavour. Out here, the flavours were simpler: sweet smoke and sweet tea. And then there was the dust. You could always taste the dust.

CHAPTER 19

In the morning, a dull orange glow had settled on the city. Rolling my motorcycle out of the hotel lobby and into the street, I clipped my plastic luggage in place before taking a good look around. Concrete buildings blocked my view of the horizon, but overhead I could see a patch of blue like faded denim on an otherwise burlap sky.

I glanced down at the map folded into the clear plastic pocket of my tank bag. There, the Euphrates River showed up as a clean blue line, but as I rode back over the water towards the highway, it appeared ugly and grey. Everything looked grey, in fact, as a hectoring wind lifted dust from the desert into the atmosphere, where it blocked out the sun. Maybe I should have turned back at that point, but here in the valley alongside the river things didn't seem so bad. After considering my options for a moment, I clicked on my left signal light and turned onto the highway, riding east.

From a nearby minaret I could hear the faint wail of the day's second call to prayer. The prayer soon faded as I rode out of range, but a circle of blue sky remained above me like a halo. I took that to be a good omen. I carried on through a hot wind that swept up from the south until I came to another town.

Rebar stuck up from flat roofs on cinderblock buildings here. Men squatted together on the ground, sipping tea from clear glasses and sheltering in the entrance of a darkened machine shop. Every street that intersected the highway was either made of dirt, or covered in dirt – one could hardly say. A row of concrete power poles ran along the main road. Their hooded street lights refused to blink on in spite of the growing darkness.

I pulled over in the lee of a building for a rationed swallow of water. With the fingers of my leather glove I brushed away the film of dust from the map pocket to see where I was, but I couldn't find this town.

I looked down the road. The concrete power poles that followed it vanished behind a curtain of earth. An unexpected shiver ran through my body. I glanced around to see if I could find a hotel, but this town was too small. There was that machine shop where the men crouched in the doorway. There was a rusty tractor parked in front of some buildings with overhead metal doors, all rolled down and locked. I couldn't stay here. Besides, it didn't feel right to quit riding for the day. There's the problem with having no destination. It's hard to stop.

Riding out of town, I crested a gentle slope, leaving the protection of the river valley. Suddenly the storm, having given fair warning, descended upon me with its entire wrath. Dust billowed in through the helmet vents, swirling about inside the visor. The edge of my nostrils caked with dirt, bringing with it that horrible dry odour that forces men of the prairies to pray. I resisted the urge to moisten my lips, but when I could bear it no more I took in a mouthful of grit that crunched against my teeth. Every movement of my body, every turn of the head, every articulation of a joint felt like scraping nails on a chalkboard. Tears rolled down my cheeks, collecting sand to deposit in the tangles of my beard. Lifting my eyes, I hoped to find comfort in my blue halo, but it was gone – buried beneath a layer of sediment.

Out here I could only see two dotted lines on the road beyond the front wheel. The needle on my speedometer touched forty kilometres per hour, but even that was too fast. For there, emerging like a villain through the fog of a nightmare, stood a monstrous tree. The brakes screamed as sand scraped between pad and rotor when I skidded to a stop. Still, I would have hit the tree if it hadn't been moving in the same direction as me.

Thank God for that. Where the thick trunk met the ground, where the roots ought to be, this tree had wheels. Now, idling behind it, I could see that this tree was really just a large vehicle spilling over with brushwood.

Peering around it with my head over the dotted line, I saw two trailers hitched to a big-wheeled tractor. As I sighted along the trailers, even the machine pulling them blurred into the storm. Aware that Syrian drivers never use their headlights, I understood the blind risk of an attempt to pass.

My headlight would never penetrate this cloud, but I switched it to high anyway before rolling on the throttle. Looking up as I passed, I saw the driver squinting into the wind, his dark robes flapping, his kafiya wrapped tightly around his head. I pulled back in front of the tractor just as an oncoming transport truck swept along, its dark mass creating turbulent eddies of sand that shook the bike. The driver flashed his lights at me, not as a warning, but to remind me that my headlight was on and that I should switch it off.

Slowing the pace after that, I kept to the centre line to avoid drifts of sand creeping in from the right. I shouldered the bike into the wind, leaning hard to resist the fate of every plastic bag that whipped across our path. Some bags snagged on low, thorny bushes where they billowed out and shredded in the wind. Others must have been carried off into Turkey. Leaning so dramatically though, the front wheel had a tendency to skip sideways, just an inch or so. Every time it happened my whole body went rigid. I slowed some more.

I reached down to pat the silver gas tank on the old bike, now marked with red pits and scratches from the sand. This storm would be hard on the machine in other ways, too. I thought about the foam air filter. By now it must be as black as a cancerous lung on a cigarette pack. I would have to soak it in gasoline tomorrow, squeezing out the dirt until it returned to the colour of butterscotch pudding. I would let it dry and then coat it with fresh oil. And the chain. That must be a mess. I would scrub every link with diesel fuel. I would adjust the tension and carefully lubricate it. I would do all of these things, I thought, and take better care of the bike in the future. First we needed to get out of this wind.

After four hours of riding, I had only gained 150 kilometres, reaching Deir ez-Zur. Ricocheting off the outskirts of the city, I caught a road that led farther inland, southwest towards the desert oasis of Palmyra.

I pulled in at a lonely fuel station outside of the city limits. After fuelling up, I parked the bike and slid out of the saddle. Stumbling forward and with shaking hand, I reached for a screen door that opened into a brick cafeteria swarming with sickly houseflies. With the brush of my arm, half a dozen of them fell from the seat, dead or unconscious. A few survivors dropped to the floor and walked away.

The snack bar had little to offer. More to the point, it had no water. I bought a blood-warm bottle of Syrian pop that only mocked my thirst. I choked down a bag of potato chips and another of dry cookies that turned to a chalky paste inside my mouth. When perhaps the last fly that could still take to the air landed on the lip of my bottle, I tried to shoo it away. Instead it dropped into the drink, dead.

I didn't feel so good myself. I sat at the table for a long

time, watching the lazy flies, listening to the screen door as it banged against the frame. Dark-haired men with thick moustaches sat around another table smoking cigarettes. People went in and out of a small prayer room off to the side, removing their shoes at the door.

I wondered what I should do. I could find a hotel if I rode into the city, but I had it in mind to reach Palmyra for night. Earlier I had spotted it on the map when I stopped to drain the last swallow of water from my bottle. On paper, Palmyra appeared as a green hollow in the desert with a pool of water surrounded by date palms. Yes, I could find shelter in the city, but from within that bleak cafeteria in the middle of a sandstorm I felt the pull of a real oasis.

Stepping back outside, I noticed that someone had washed the dust off every light on my motorcycle. I found no one to thank.

Judging from the map, Palmyra was at least as far away as I had just come, but the road no longer followed the river. It stretched through an unpopulated land. As I started up the bike, I still didn't know if I would carry on or find a hotel in the city. I threw a leg over, pulled in the clutch and kicked the bike into gear. Rolling along the gravel parking lot, weighing my options, I came to the highway. Finally the machine leaned left, southwest into the sand, towards Palmyra.

Visibility had improved and I could hold the bike almost straight up. Shadowy camels walked beside the road and I could see three or four dotted lines ahead of me. Off to the side I saw men with a cache of weapons. They had a heavy gun mounted to their truck, and several rifles leaned up against the front bumper, presumably used for patrolling the Iraqi border. The men, wrapped in kafiyas to guard against the blowing dust, turned to watch me pass. One of them stood, as if he meant to follow. But they stayed put.

Then, just as suddenly as if someone had turned off a tap, the wind stopped. I could see to the edge of the earth as the beige desert spread out to meet a watercolour sky. Wisps of cloud hung in the air like cigarette smoke and low hills rolled on the horizon. I lifted the visor for the first time that day to breathe in clean air. The sun was before me now, splintering off scratches in my sunglasses and casting a long shadow behind me.

My eyelids grew heavy and I felt myself slump forward onto the tank bag a bit. Pulling off the road onto the flat, hard surface of the land, I rode out about a mile until I came to a dry riverbed. After riding down into it, I switched off the bike. If only I had water. It was the wrong season for flash floods, so I could set up camp right there. No one could see me from the highway. But I had no water. I needed to reach Palmyra before nightfall. That was my last thought as I lay down in the shade of the motorcycle to sleep.

The next morning I awoke in Palmyra with just a blurry memory of how I got there. The sun had been setting as I rode into town. I remembered taking a desperate drink of water and then dropping into bed, too tired to wash off the dust. I didn't sleep much. For most of the night I rocked forward onto my knees, kneeling in bed with my head on the pillow to keep from vomiting.

For several days I would remain sick and lethargic. Even so, when I woke in Palmyra that first morning, I was at peace. A call to prayer carried on the gentle breeze, ruffling the thin white curtain as it pushed through my open window. I lay in bed, listening to the muezzin sing his adhan. I smiled. This was it. At least for the moment, I had found my destination.

CHAPTER 20

In the morning, I rode up a steep hill to the base of a stone fortress that commanded sweeping views in every direction. The land was jagged and uniformly brown to the west, comprised of hills that one could almost call mountains. To the south, I looked down upon a wide valley dotted with square towers built long ago to house the dead. And looking east, there was Palmyra.

The town abutted the ruins of an ancient city with a colonnade that doglegged into a green oasis of date palms and pomegranate trees. Though most guidebooks proclaim these ruins to be Syria's pre-eminent tourist attraction, I was more interested in the trees – I didn't have a guidebook, remember.

As the sun worked its way down through a hazy sky, I watched the desert scroll from beige to yellow and gold, then crimson, before slipping into purple shadows. The lights came on against the castle wall and I rode back down to the hotel.

Walking to the oasis in the morning, I ended up paying admission to the Temple of Bel upon recommendation from a Swiss tourist. With no guidebook to explain the ruins, I spent a few extra dollars for an eager guide to show me around. Mohammed claimed to have a doctorate in archaeology, and he seemed knowledgeable enough about Bel. A thick man with dark skin, Mohammed spoke in a rich baritone, like James Earl Jones with an Arabic accent. "That's the Phoenician god," he said. "Not to be confused with Baal, the god of the Babylonians."

Mohammed pointed out the place where priests would have made sacrifices to Bel. "And here," he said, "is where the blood would flow. They sacrificed cattle, goats, and sheep. But no pigs." He smiled. "Do you know why no pigs?"

"Because they are unclean."

"Exactly. Does that sound familiar?"

I nodded. It seemed to be the consensus in the region still. Mohammed highlighted other similarities between what the Phoenicians believed early in the Common Era and what other monotheistic religions believe to this day. I got the impression that he thought it was all hooey.

Still in the courtyard, Mohammed pointed up at the temple itself – a rectangular structure of limestone on a stepped foundation. Ridged columns with ornate capitals encircled the building, in various states of preservation.

"Once it would have supported a roof of polished gold and bronze," he said. "When the sun shone upon it, it could be seen up to seventy kilometres away. It would serve as a beacon, like a lighthouse to those in the desert."

"I like that," I said as I turned to look at the next thing. "A lighthouse in the desert. That's cool."

That wasn't the reaction Mohammed wanted. Apparently, he felt that I should be rather much more impressed.

"That's amazing technology," Mohammed persisted. "It's better than Canadian technology," he boasted. "Better than German."

I nodded, still sort of impressed. "Yeah, but … we're still talking about a shiny roof, right?"

After that Mohammed didn't bother with the roof.

"Next," he announced boldly, "I will show you big asses."

"What?"

"Big asses."

"That's what I thought you said."

"You know big asses?"

I nodded, "Yeah..."

"The flying horse?"

"Oh, Pegasus. Yeah, I didn't know where you were going with that."

And so he continued the tour, pointing out details on various reliefs with the aid of a mirror that he used to reflect the sun, like a laser pointer. Back at the gift shop he invited me for tea with some of his colleagues before I left to explore the oasis.

To avoid the distinction of becoming the only tourist in history to visit Palmyra without seeing the archaeological marvel of its colonnade, I rode past the ruins in the morning on the way out of town. I had intended to park the bike and walk around for a few minutes, snapping ho-hum obligatory photos, but my eyes lit up when I saw two locals and their tiny motorcycles on the ancient path. Suddenly I had a better idea. Backtracking a bit, I found a spot where I could just squeeze the Oscillator between two boulders to gain access to the site. I rode along the gravel walkway between limestone pillars before parking beneath a towering archway. Perhaps I'd find archaeology more interesting if I could view every site in this manner, especially the museums.

The modern road leading out of Palmyra had its own appeal. It was straight and smooth. I enjoyed the clean lines of the desert and the bluebird sky. Camels plodded along the roadside, and I could see more Bedouin tents. Mostly, I was just happy to see.

Passing through Homs, I continued west towards the Mediterranean, riding very near the Lebanese border. There was a castle of some note in the area. The castle, Krak des Chevaliers, was often described as being out of a "childhood fantasy." It seemed odd that everyone should use that exact phrase, until I learned that it was described that way in virtually every guidebook. The description was attributed to writer Paul Theroux.

Turning away from the main road, I continued north up a strip of asphalt that climbed steeply into the hills. When I rounded the final corner to see the fortress perched atop a hill, I could tell right away that Paul Theroux had nailed it. The white stone walls with their smooth drum towers looked elegant and formidable. Not one corbel or ashlar block appeared broken or misaligned on the outer wall, and the talus wall beyond that looked just as smooth as it sloped down and out of sight. Except for tufts of vegetation growing in the mortar between blocks, one might have thought it was still occupied by a crusader garrison. The whole structure flickered beneath a moody sky.

Dreams of dragons and damsels leaped to mind as I entered the castle, and I found it difficult to walk up any of the dozen spiral staircases – I had to run. I could almost smell the hay in the stables or hear the clang of metal in the armoury. Stooped low through an arched corridor, I peered through every arrow loop with my imaginary bow before emerging into the courtyard. There I found a series of Gothic arches with a vaulted ceiling that led me in the direction of the chapel.

There was nothing special about the chapel. It was just a dim room with a high-arched ceiling. A squat *mimbar* of smooth stone attested that Muslims occupied the building after the Crusaders had gone. It sat in a pool of grey light that filtered in from the entrance. I stood there for a moment as I whispered a short prayer. I didn't give it much thought, though, and it's quite possible that the prayer never left the room. If so, I like to think it hangs in the air still, trapped with a million others in an invisible cloud that grows with the centuries.

Next I set out to find the highest spot on the tallest tower. Emerging from a narrow staircase, I found myself on top of the castle at last. With no guardrail, or even so much as a warning sign to prevent visitors from toppling to their deaths, this tower would be a coddling mother's worst nightmare.

From here I could look down into the stagnant moat choked with green algae on one side and into the courtyard on the other. Looking south, I could also see for miles down into Lebanon and, in every other direction, the stepped farmland and white villages of the Syrian landscape. The location of the castle made perfect sense. From here one could see advancing armies long before they arrived, possibly days before. And that's basically what happened in the twelfth century, when the few remaining Crusaders still holding the fort found themselves surrounded by vast Muslim armies. Though well provisioned to withstand a siege of many years, the embattled garrison surrendered the castle without a fight, in exchange for safe passage to the Mediterranean.

Actually, they fell for a clever forgery supposedly written by their superiors in Tripoli, Lebanon, allowing them to surrender. The letter was really written by a Mamluk sultan, but the crusaders only learned of the trickery after they had handed him the gate keys and arrived safely at the sea. Of course, by that time it was too late to do anything. Presumably the sultan had already moved in all his stuff.

While I took a final walk along the ramparts, a cold fog rolled in and it started to drizzle. Winter hours were in effect anyway, and the castle would soon be closing.

I walked back to the hotel, just a stone's throw away. I anticipated a long night. Besides the castle, which was now closed at four in the afternoon, the hotel with its four or five rooms was the only building in the area, and I its only guest.

Or so I thought. Then I heard a familiar voice. "Welcome!" the man shouted. I looked up to see a tall man in a baseball hat and glasses. It was Raj, the Swiss tourist who I had met in Palmyra.

"We have a decision to make!" he shouted. When I got to the hotel he explained.

"How much are you paying for your room?" he asked.

"Well," I chuckled, "I'm no sucker. They wanted ten dollars, but the place is empty, right? It took me a while, but I talked him down to seven."

"The guidebook says it should be five."

That wiped the smirk off my face.

Even so, Raj seemed impressed. He hadn't done much better, and haggling was his thing. I had watched him argue about the price of everything in Palmyra, even the posted standard prices of meals in restaurants. He fought fiercely, raising his voice and making a scene even after the price had already dropped several times. Then, after the waiter had finally given us his best offer, Raj would add, "Oh, and of course we'll expect a free narghile afterwards."

Raj insisted on paying what the locals would pay, and he very nearly did. He felt it his duty to haggle for the sake of travellers who followed behind.

"Otherwise," he said, "the price ratchets up until the tourist pays him a week's salary for every meal."

Of course, he had a point. Prices are flexible in the

Middle East and merchants capitalize on the fact that most tourists hate conflict. Raj, however, seemed to take it a bit far.

"I only got him down to seven dollars as well," he said. "But if we share a room we can each pay six, which is quite good, I think."

It seems absurd to sacrifice privacy to save one single dollar, but on the road a dollar means so much more. Raj dropped his pack on the unclaimed bed in my room and we left for supper.

CHAPTER 21

With the heavy cloud cover and spattering rain, darkness fell upon the hotel even before the sun had set. The restaurant windows overlooking the castle turned into dark mirrors. Given our isolated position and the poor weather, there was nothing for us to do but order another narghile, our second of the evening. When that pipe expired I decided to do some bike maintenance.

The Oscillator had a slow leak on the rear tire. It wasn't a big deal, really. It just meant that I had to top it up with air about twice a week. I had an electric compressor to do the job, but it seemed to be getting less efficient lately. I figured I should pull the pump apart to see if I could find the problem.

With plenty of time and good working conditions, I actually looked forward to the project. Ever since reading *Zen and the Art of Motorcycle Maintenance* I've tried to emulate Robert Pirsig's approach to working on motorcycles and, to a lesser extent, his approach to life. Of course, I seldom measure up to his standards, but I do try. When possible, I work slowly, deliberately. The key is to take your time, do things right. That's the Pirsig way.

I laid out all the tools I would need as Raj looked on.

"You must know a lot about mechanics to travel this way," he noted.

"Well, I'm no mechanic," I said, "but I do know enough to get by."

I nudged a screwdriver into place within the neat line of tools on the ground and smiled. *Yeah, I thought, I'm getting better at this stuff, and there's nothing like the satisfaction of a job done well.*

An hour later, I had smashed the compressor to bits in a fit of rage. My tools were scattered along a twenty-metre path between my room and the motorcycle, and the bike had a perfectly flat tire. As a kind of stupidity bonus, it was the *front* tire that had gone flat. Instead of risking a test of my repair job on a leaking tire, I had drained the good one.

Raj no longer assumed that one had to be mechanically inclined to travel by motorcycle. Having witnessed the tantrum, he now sat on his bed, somewhat reluctant to speak.

To calm down, I reached for my camera and began snapping photos of the room like a crime scene photographer. That cleared the emotion – everything appears antiseptic through a viewfinder.

After putting my camera away, I replayed the events of the past hour in my mind. I could understand how I had destroyed the pump – I risk breaking the very machine I try to fix every time I brandish tools – but how had I managed to flatten my front tire? It was an innocent bystander. Collateral damage.

Mostly, I recalled the sounds: the cork-pop of the pump's pressure gauge when it shot past my head. The hiss of air rushing out of the tire and the funny squeak it made when I pressed my thumb against the open valve. It all happened quite fast. Even so, I didn't drain the air from the tire all at once. Oh, no. That took two tries.

"Maybe you should wait until you have a backup air

supply," suggested Raj after watching me drain most of the air on my first test.

Raj didn't know me that well. When I get locked onto something, I never stop to think things through midway. Screw Robert Pirsig.

I patched up the pump as best I could and returned to the bike. I knew that the one-way air valve was missing – it had disappeared into the darkness along with the pressure gauge – but that shouldn't matter. As long as the compressor generated more PSI than what remained in the tire, it should work just fine.

It was a gamble, but I figured I had nothing to lose. In hindsight, I could lose whatever air remained in the tire. And when I heard the sickening noise of the compressor's push-rod snap in two, that's exactly what happened. Unable to re-move the attachment from my wheel fast enough, and with no one-way valve to prevent it, I watched the tire fall com-pletely flat. The rim came to rest on a few millimetres of rub-ber. I had killed it.

I walked quietly back to the room and smashed the pump all to hell.

CHAPTER 22

It would be a frustrating morning. Not only did I have to in-
flate my tire somehow, but I had no Syrian cash. I had nothing left after paying for my room and, with my bike down, I
had no way to reach a bank.

While I scratched my head over the problem, Raj fixed
everything. He got the hotel manager to make some phone
calls, and soon a rusty Payloader bounced its way up the
driveway towards my bike. A serious-looking man with a
moustache and grubby work clothes climbed out of the cab.
He went straight to work uncoiling an air hose. Raj, who
knew that I was out of money, discreetly handed me a few
hundred Syrian pounds – the equivalent of around four
dollars.

"He'll want money," Raj said quietly. We both knew that.

The man did not have the proper air chuck with him, so
he unscrewed the valve stem, managing to fill the tire with
just a straight hose. He never spoke. When he had finished
putting the hose away, he shook my hand, walked back to his
machine, and drove off.

"Wow. That's a nice surprise," I said. "When I stopped by
the highway yesterday to photograph some camels, this guy
pulls up behind me and starts demanding that I pay him – for
taking pictures of the camels!"

"Did you?" asked Raj.

"What, pay him? Of course not. But he got really mad." I held the Syrian pounds out for Raj.

"Keep it," he said. "It's only a few dollars. It's nothing. And you need it."

I laughed. "I've seen you fight to save way less than this."

"I know. That's so we don't get cheated. And because I've saved that money in the past, I can give it away to help a friend, see? Us travellers, we have to stick together."

Raj left to view the castle while I packed up my things. As I rode past the fortress, I looked up and saw him. He stood on the highest point of the tallest tower waving down to me. He pumped both fists in the air and I nodded. Paul Theroux was right about that castle.

The temperature warmed as the road dropped down into Damascus. Before hitting the worst of the traffic, I stopped at the edge of the city for a sip of water and a small package of stale cookies that I found in my tank bag. Raj had given me directions for a hostel near the old city, but they were walking directions. First I needed to get close with my bike.

I strapped up my helmet. With that, the friendly sun turned angry, beating down on me as I navigated dusty streets. When at last I found the Citadel of Damascus, I had barely enough saliva left to wet my lips. I couldn't pinpoint my location on the map, and with no safe place to pull over, the traffic carried me away. I swore inside my helmet. I spent another hour pushing through congested streets back to the white castle walls where I had begun.

Arriving the second time, I edged over on the road against a metal railing to examine the map. Of course, it only confirmed that I had found the old city. It had no hotels marked, and until I could park the bike to walk, I couldn't even try to find one. Wishing only for a cool shower, I faced the fact that I had to keep riding. Getting swept away by traffic once again, I fought for another hour just to make my way back to the citadel.

At that point I nearly flipped Damascus the bird. Who needs it? It would have been easier to ride south towards Jordan, but just then I managed to squeeze off the road to park on a busy sidewalk. I didn't bother with the directions Raj had given me for the hostel, though. I didn't know where I was in relation to his starting point – and anyway, I would take anything. Within five minutes, I found the exact hostel Raj had suggested. I checked in immediately.

CHAPTER 23

According to legend, when the Prophet Mohammed first
saw Damascus he refused to enter the city because he only
wanted to enter paradise one time, when he died. Based on
that information it's safe to assume that he wouldn't hesitate
to enter the city if he saw it today. Looking down on it from
a ridge, Damascus is a dollop of hummus mashed into a shallow bread bowl. Its five million people have sprawled out
into a landscape of short buildings beneath a brown dome
of smog.

The city had nearly spit me out with its congested traffic the day before and, on first impressions, I wouldn't have
missed much if that had happened. Now that I was up close,
I could see Damascus for the charmer it was.

My bike leaned up against the outside of my hotel on
a narrow street of smooth paving stones. Red and yellow
plastic chairs spilled into the road from a dozen open-air tea-
shops, where young Syrians, both male and female, gathered
alongside grubby backpackers to smoke narghile and play
backgammon. Teenaged waiters hustled through the crowd,
swinging metal baskets filled with hot coals for the pipes and
trays suspended from wire frames covered with clear cups of
mint tea.

From there, it was a short walk to the old city. There
were always a few dirty children and one man with a badly

broken leg begging on the busy pedestrian overpass that I used. Usually I tossed a few coins into one basket or another as I walked by, high above the stream of honking yellow taxis and lime-green buses crammed with passengers. Down the stairs, I dodged through a street market of trinkets and cigarettes, then over the grey water of the Barada River. The river is ancient, and it may have been the one that the leprous Naaman wanted to use to cure his disease instead of the Jordan River as instructed by the Prophet Elisha, but now it moves through the city collecting garbage. Bathing in that would only make you sicker.

From there I walked along the white stone wall of the citadel, beneath a billboard of President Bashar al-Assad that read, "Syria Believes in You" (other posters depicted him with Hezbollah leader Hassan Nasrallah), and into a wide corridor overarched by a metal roof where shafts of light poured through old bullet holes.

This was Souq al-Hamidiyya. Two-storey shops dating back to the nineteenth century lined both sides of the market. A man with a silver coffee pot clinked porcelain cups together like a bell with his fingers. Vendors pushed wooden carts loaded with candy and nuts, toys, and tourist kitsch along the cobbled road.

I walked straight to Bekdach, an ice cream parlour that served up mastic ice cream. Pushing through the crowd, I ordered a large cone with pistachios while behind the counter a team of men in white shirts and rubber gloves worked the ice cream. One pounded it down in a large silver vat using a long wooden paddle. Another scooped it out of an adjacent barrel, slapping it into a waffle cone before handing it off to another man, who rolled it through shaved pistachios.

Mastic ice cream bridges the gap between ice cream and taffy. You can lick it like ice cream, but it has a subtle, chewy texture. It can be rolled and shaped. It gets this quality from gum mastic, a resin that weeps from mastic shrubs, found throughout the Mediterranean region. Other ingredients may include cardamom and rosewater, but to me it tasted like vanilla. Once I discovered it, I had at least one serving every day. With cone in hand, I would lose myself in a web of narrow lanes overhung with spreading vines and Ottoman-era apartments braced on sagging wooden beams.

That's how I passed a few listless days in Damascus, still recovering from the bug I had picked up along the ride into Palmyra. When I wasn't wandering in the old city, I was bent over my notebook, drafting elaborate flowcharts to narrow down my options.

Every path ended with Canada and, to be honest, the shortest line to that end appealed the most. I was tired. I had failed to accomplish what I had set out to do, and every direction from Syria seemed contrived. The only elegant line that jumped out on a map was the one that terminated in South Africa, but I didn't have the money for that. If I tried to make it go, I would have to ship the bike home from whatever country I ended up in when I went broke.

Flying home from Israel looked to be the easiest option, largely because I knew people there who could help with language problems. In the end, though, I decided that I would regret it if I rushed home. I selected a line on my flowchart that ran through Lebanon.

CHAPTER 24

Beirut should have been just a short ride to the west, so when the directions I got took me north, back towards Krak de Chevaliers, I spun around and rode back against the flow on a busy highway. Soon I located the airport, a landmark precisely on the opposite end of town from the road to Beirut. Having already spent several hours coughing up diesel smoke, I abandoned the systematic search for Lebanon, choosing instead to follow the very next road that pointed west. Thirty seconds later, that road directed me straight to the border.

Once inside Lebanon, I bought local currency from a half dozen slick-haired men in tight shirts. They had nice shoes, too. Their quick talk and lightning math left me scratching my head. When they had gone, I stood around trying to figure out what happened. I stayed there so long that some of them returned.

"Are you all right?" they said.

"Yeah. I'm just doing the math."

"Do you want to exchange more money?"

"Uh, not until I figure out how badly you guys screwed me over."

They laughed and scattered like cockroaches.

As it turned out, I did get a reasonable rate, which is why I had to check the figure so many times.

That can't be right, I kept thinking. *But that's almost the proper exchange.*

You'll have to forgive my cynicism. It's just that I've crossed a few borders and I've lost a lot of money. Math is not my thing, and I seldom show up prepared with a calculator or even, for that matter, any knowledge of what the exchange rate should be. Instead, when the money-changers present their first offer, I just give an indignant snort. If the offer improves, I shrug. Then I frown, sometimes with a thoughtful nod. Finally I accept whatever they give me. This strategy has resulted in many a late-night tantrum after learning the actual exchange rate. In any case, it paid off this time.

With no map to guide me, every fork in the road was a gamble. I chose the branch that approximated west every time, hoping that I would bump into the Mediterranean, but with the sun hidden behind clouds I lost my bearings and had to choose blind. When a bridge construction project forced me onto a bypass that dropped into a gully, I decided to ask a construction worker for directions.

Unfortunately, I was slow to piece together just exactly why the bridge needed repair. When I pulled over to ask a worker for help, I found myself facing the last man I would ever wish to impose upon. The same instinct that warns a traveller to avoid photographing bridges, soldiers, and government buildings in a country still reeling from war should also keep one from approaching soldiers at a bombed-out bridge. Looking up, I could see twisted rebar from a large section of concrete that had been blasted away during the 2006 July War with Israel, about sixteen months earlier.

Stupid, stupid, Jeremy, I thought as I took off my helmet, but it was too late to do anything else. Though he never spoke one English word, the soldier made it very clear that he was not a tour guide. He pointed to his heavily armed co-workers, suggesting that I leave his sphere of influence with all haste, which I did.

Tensions were high in Lebanon for several reasons. The July War, or Summer War, between Hezbollah and Israel was fresh in the people's collective memory, and the blood had barely been washed from the streets in a more recent conflict between the Lebanese armed forces and Fatah al-Islam, a Sunni militant group. Rolling blackouts still remained throughout Lebanon to remind everyone of that battle. But what really had people on edge were whispers of potential violence over the upcoming parliamentary elections.

Of the three key positions within the Lebanese government, each one is allocated for a particular religious group. The speaker must be a Shia Muslim, the prime minister a Sunni, and the president a Maronite Christian. The problems inherent in that arrangement have grown worse over the years as the demography of Lebanon shifts, leaving certain groups under-represented while minorities have more power than perhaps they should.

The term of current president Émile Lahoud was drawing to a close, and a suitable replacement had yet to be found. Lahoud's successor needed support from two-thirds of parliament, but Hezbollah, a significant Shia presence in Lebanese politics, balked at every candidate, promising to boycott elections. If parliament went ahead and elected a president anyway, Hezbollah would not recognize his authority. Although no one knew exactly what would happen in this scenario, everyone agreed that it would be bad.

Anyway, who would want the job of president under those circumstances? Political assassinations occur with alarming frequency in Lebanon. (Either that, or there are a lot of cars out there with faulty wiring systems that cause accidental, if convenient, catastrophic explosions.)

Following every political death, fingers point in one of two directions. Either people blame Iran and Syria on one side, or they blame Israel and the United States on the other. In the end, blame generally rests on whoever benefits from the assassination, but even that is hard to gauge.

The road descended in curves through green hills dotted by white houses, before looping past chain restaurants like McDonald's and KFC as it neared Beirut. The road may have been designed for two lanes of traffic, or possibly three, but that hardly mattered. People passed at will, around corners, blind, madly jostling for position. If you waited for a safe opportunity to overtake, others viewed it as a sign of weakness and overtook you.

At last I could see the Mediterranean. I was safely in Beirut. The city sparkled more than the water, with its tall buildings of glass and steel, bright Italian sports cars, and the tight shiny shirts of the men inside them. After the conservative feel of Aleppo and Damascus, the women stood out all the more in their form-fitting clothes and short skirts. That was the case, at least, in certain parts of town.

Beirut is schizophrenic. It has upscale shopping malls with jewellery stores and valet parking just a few blocks from suburbs plagued with poverty and religious fundamentalism. It has trendy bars pulsing with music and young, sweaty bodies. It has the Corniche, a paved walkway with palm trees that wraps around a curving bay along the Mediterranean. There's a Hard Rock Cafe and a McDonald's on one end, and a ramshackle amusement park with a Ferris wheel on the other. Then it has abandoned high-rise buildings spackled with bullet holes from the long civil war in the seventies and eighties.

I found a three-storey hostel just a few blocks uphill from the wharf. They had no vacancy when I arrived, but for four dollars they let me sleep on the roof beneath a billboard that read, "Roadster Diner – There goes my heart." The hostel catered mostly to fake reporters, a handful of actual reporters, and a menagerie of squinty people who thought they were spies.

CHAPTER 25

The white porcelain cup clinked against the saucer when I put it down. Stirring sugar into expensive cappuccino, I tapped the spoon on the rim before placing it on the smooth table. My laptop whirred to life. I had just returned from a day of wandering and I wanted to do some research on a certain part of the city.

The mezzanine coffee shop looked down onto an orderly room filled with rows of books. As music played, one could easily forget that this Virgin Megastore was in the heart of a troubled Middle Eastern city. It could have been anywhere. A clean, well-lighted place. Not quite the same as the one Hemingway wrote about, but it would do.

I typed "Sabra, Shatila refugee camp" into the search engine to find pages of material, mainly chronicling one infamous event. I sipped my coffee.

Earlier, I had stumbled out of a crowded minibus into the poor Beirut neighbourhood of Sabra, near a bustling fruit market. A man wearing foam sandals pushed a wooden cart loaded with bright oranges. I stood against a wall for a moment to get my bearings, doing my best to look inconspicuous, a decidedly difficult task for me in that part of the city.

I had no agenda, really. I merely wanted to see one of the Palestinian camps that I had heard mention of in the news.

When they learned that I wanted to visit Shatila, the hostel owners wrote out some directions for the driver in Arabic. They warned me against taking pictures unless I had explicit permission from everyone who would appear in the shot. They also warned against acting like an idiot tourist and told me I should probably not linger there after dark.

This part of the city didn't look too bad, but I hadn't entered the camp yet. Neighbouring Shatila was established as a temporary refuge for Palestinians fleeing the 1948 Arab-Israeli War, but it has a distinct air of sad permanence now. Following the directions, I began walking. I couldn't put my finger on the exact moment when I crossed into Shatila, but when I saw a man standing in a puddle of stagnant water to fiddle with a nest of arcing electrical wires, I knew I was there.

The wires ran everywhere in tangles that reached up to buildings and down to the ground. Corridors of broken pavement squeezed between tall buildings that denied them a place in the sun. Where the alleys widened enough to accommodate a sidewalk, they also hosted piles of trash.

The apartment buildings were grey. Some of them were finished in rough concrete while others had exposed cinderblocks with cracked mortar. Faded posters featuring the Palestinian flag and former PLO leader Yasser Arafat broke the monotony, as did the laundry that hung from balconies.

When I stopped to look at a particularly messy web of wires, an old man with a thin beard approached and asked if I wanted something.

"Where are you from?" I asked.

"Haifa," he replied. I knew that Palestinians in these camps claim to originate from wherever their forefathers lived in what has now become Israel, even if they and their parents were born in the camps. In this case, though, the man might have actually left Haifa in 1948 as a toddler.

The people of Shatila live in a cage, of sorts. They cannot return to Palestine. They cannot integrate into Lebanon. By government order, they are restricted to certain privileges and job opportunities outside the camp. They are trapped, a people with no country and faint hope.

I walked through the streets in silence as I tried to take it all in, the squalor, the bleak existence. I wanted to know more about the bullet holes in the walls, the cramped facilities, and Shatila's haggard people. With darkness approaching, I took the minibus back to familiar ground, where I read online accounts of the Shatila massacre in 1982, perpetrated by a Lebanese Christian Phalangist militia with the support of the Israeli Defense Forces. The IDF blocked all exits to the camp and allowed the Christian Phalanges to enter under the pretext of rooting out remaining members of the PLO. What seemed like a legitimate operation on the surface turned ugly as both Phalanges and Israelis far outstepped their bounds.

It was a massacre. Though the number of casualties is hotly disputed, it ranges from several hundred to several thousand. Naturally, opinions vary regarding culpability as well, but when Israeli citizens learned of the slaughter they took to their own streets in protest. As a result, the Knesset organized an investigation that found the Israeli defence minister, Ariel Sharon, personally responsible. Mr. Sharon later went on to become the prime minister of Israel.

The last swallow of coffee had gone cold by the time I switched off the computer and clicked the lid shut. I rubbed my eyes and buried my face in my hands. After all that reading it seemed like a supremely bad idea to have gone directly from a Palestinian camp to a Virgin Megastore.

Disheartened, I trudged back through Martyr's Square, pausing before a bronze statue of four figures, all torn through with bullet holes. So many people have died in this region over the years. The more I thought about it, the harder it became to distinguish between the good guys and the bad guys. Such terms require extensive qualification. Perhaps they don't even apply.

After each round of violence, no matter who initiates it, someone invariably points out how many innocent civilians died. But that's a grey area, too. Right and wrong, innocent and guilty, it's all measured on a sliding scale. In a place and time where most people harbour hatred, how can you tell if anyone is innocent?

CHAPTER 26

Raindrops fell to earth that night like heavy ball bearings as an electrical storm shook the city. I lay shivering on the roof beneath a small tarpaulin I had found in the hallway. I hugged my knees tight to my chest. A few seconds after the first lightning bolt rent the sky, I wondered whether I could distinguish between the sound of thunder and the sound of bombs. If I heard an explosion, what should I do? Probably the same thing I should do anyway because of the lightning. I tucked the tarp in a little tighter around my body.

Around one o'clock in the morning, a few friends came up to the roof to check on me. They cracked the door open and, after they had mostly finished laughing, one of them shouted, "Jeremy! Are you all right? You should come inside, man! Sleep on the floor if you have to."

"Yeah, well, if it gets any worse I will," I hollered back, though the only way it could have got worse was if lightning actually struck the metal billboard above my head – a highly probable scenario, now that I think about it. "I'm OK under here, but I'm definitely taking a room first thing in the morning!"

Everyone seemed on edge that night, and not just because of the weather. The thunder sounded too much like their worst fears for the city. In the morning, I noticed many bloodshot eyes.

President Lahoud would step down by the end of the week, on Friday, yet parliament bickered on about a successor. Elections were scheduled for the next day, a Wednesday, but they had been postponed several times already. It looked as though they would be postponed again. No one could say what would happen if Lahoud left behind him an empty office, but one Jordanian man in our hostel believed he had a good idea.

Hearing commotion from the common room in the morning, I walked downstairs to see the man pacing, shouting hysterically in Arabic. Eventually he slumped into a chair where he rocked back and forth, holding his head between his hands as if in a vise. After resting for a moment in this manner, if you could call it resting, he stood to resume shouting, mostly at Zaher, the hostel owner.

Zaher stood behind his desk with a telephone pressed to his ear and a concerned look on his face. Occasionally he glanced up, tapping the air with his free hand as though patting an invisible dog. The man would not calm down. The coattails of his suit jacket flapped behind him as he spun and rushed from the room, practically screaming.

"What's going on?" I said.

"He thinks we're all going to die," said Drew. Drew said this without looking up from his copy of the *Daily Star*. He took a sip of beer.

The big American wore his grey baseball cap backwards. Drew had the look of a friendly college linebacker – the sort of man who wouldn't hurt you unless you did something incredibly stupid to provoke him, in which case he very, very easily could. Drew was one of the unfortunate few who, like me, had shown up in Lebanon not because he wanted to witness the elections but merely for a lovely holiday. He had been oblivious to any political tension before he arrived. He took news of the current situation in stride.

"I see. All going to die," I muttered as I popped the top off my own beer and sat down opposite him.

"What do you think?" I said.

Drew didn't answer, because just then the Jordanian man blustered into the room to commence shouting. Drew put down his paper to watch the spectacle.

Zaher's brother Wissam sat in the corner with his head in his hands. He finally looked up, wide-eyed. The Jordanian wasn't exactly doing wonders for morale.

"Wissam, what's he saying?" I asked.

"He thinks he'll die," said Wissam with a quiver in his voice. "He wants to flee the country before tomorrow's election, but he can't find a way out. Zaher is trying now."

Maybe the thunder spooked him, or maybe this man had actually seen war.

Whenever he looked in my direction I flashed a reassuring smile, but it never registered. I don't think he could see anything through those wild eyes. I turned to Drew.

"What do you want to do today?" I said.

Drew popped the cap off another bottle of beer. He waited for a break in the shouting to reply. "Well, what can we do in this rain? We could go to the museum," he suggested.

"Yeah, I'd be up for that. Maybe on the way back we swing through Haret Hreik, if the weather clears."

"What?" said Drew. "I can't hear you above this guy."

I walked over and sat down beside Drew. "Haret Hreik," I said again. "It's a part of the city that got flattened last summer during the war. It's a Hezbollah hotspot. Wissam told me about it."

Wissam nodded. By this time Zaher had found a

solution for the Jordanian man. The man hurried out to pack his things while Zaher followed him out, shaking his head.

"If you go, you must not take any photographs," warned Wissam. "If you do, maybe someone takes your camera, or maybe they just delete the photos, but it's best not to try."

"But, is it OK for two white guys with no Arabic to just wander around?" I asked.

Wissam thought for a moment. "I think, yes," he said. "Just no photos."

"Sounds interesting," said Drew.

The rain let up by the time we had finished with the National Museum of Beirut, although tendrils of cloud still reached down to touch the rooftops. Drew and I stepped from the taxi in Haret Hreik to look around.

Another chaotic web of wires hung between iron light posts and balcony railings, just like in Shatila, but the roads weren't as crowded and they had nicer cars. Picking our way around puddles on a muddy road, Drew and I came upon a crater filled with rubble. Presumably, a group of apartments had once stood here. Much of the debris had been removed, but there still remained a lot of work to do before anyone could rebuild. The concrete and cinderblock housing units on the edge of the blast zone escaped without serious damage, except for one ten-storey building that caught my eye. It looked as if a giant scalpel had sheared it down the middle. Several floors had only three of four walls on the outer rooms, allowing you to look right inside from the street.

A few walls remained intact on other levels, but those that had once looked in on a family room now faced out towards a hole in the ground. A brown chest of drawers balanced on a stub of concrete that projected from the sixth floor. Next to it, hanging on a pink bedroom wall, was a painting of the ocean in a gold picture frame.

When Drew and I darted beneath the overhang in front of a shop to shelter from a light rain, a man came out to invite us for tea. We sat down on plastic chairs in a cold room with three men. The men were all smoking and huddled before an old television. They seemed interested in us, but we could hardly communicate. Instead, we all sipped our tea while watching the incomprehensible movie *Duel*.

A young man walked into the room. He stiffened when he noticed Drew and me. The man was dressed in black all the way down to his shit-kicking boots. He had dark hair and a neatly trimmed beard. He took a cup of tea and sat quietly in the corner as we all turned back to the movie. Out of the corner of my eye, I noticed a friend of the man motioning at me to get my attention. When I looked over, he pointed to the man in black as if shooting him with a gun and whispered, "Terrorist."

That created an awkward moment.

All eyes turned to the man in black, who suddenly resembled a deer in headlights. He feigned laughter: "Ha, ha, ha." Then he chided his friend in Arabic before making his exit.

I don't know what made the man in black so uncomfortable. He obviously supported Hezbollah, but who in that district did not? Perhaps he had fought against Israel in the Summer War. In fact, I assume he did. Still, what could I do about it? Should I have thrown him into a headlock until someone from the CIA showed up?

Drew and I finished our tea, thanked our hosts, and returned to the hostel.

CHAPTER 27

I walked downtown in the morning. Sitting on a stone ledge opposite the parliament building, I looked up at a clock tower. It stood in the centre of a pedestrian circle paved with dark bricks. Putting my coffee down beside me, I scanned lead stories in the newspaper. There were no explosions. No gunshots. Parliament had postponed elections again until Friday, the very day that Lahoud would vacate his position.

I walked back to the hostel through empty streets. Since its virtual destruction during Lebanon's long civil war, the downtown core has undergone major restoration. It's beautiful and clean. Except it feels artificial. Buildings look old, but they are uniformly faced with cream-coloured blocks that have yet to soften with wind or rain. Walking past the Mohammed al-Amin Mosque, I reached out to touch the wall. It bounced back a hollow thud as I rapped it with my knuckles. They should have at least made the mosque out of solid stone, I thought. Like the rest of downtown, it was just a facade.

Stepping around concrete barriers ringed with razor wire, I navigated Tent City, a massive sit-in spearheaded by Hezbollah. It began after the Summer War, in protest against then-Prime Minister Fouad Siniora, but it failed to accomplish its objectives. What had once been a thriving community of supporters now mainly comprised empty tents with an occasional group huddled before a small fire. I just liked walking through the checkpoints.

Beirut breathed a sigh of relief when nothing happened on Wednesday, but come Friday everyone held their breath again. Elections were slated for the afternoon, but they were postponed. Lahoud stepped down at midnight, leaving Lebanon without a president. He declared a state of emergency as his last act, but he couldn't get the prime minister on board to make it official. Regardless, armoured personnel carriers rolled into Beirut as the army ramped up its presence.

Sensitive to the people's fear over the precarious situation, politicians uttered reassurances to the press that they would not make any major decisions until they could agree on a compromise presidential candidate. The press called it organized emptiness. One paper even published a blank photo frame on the front page where a picture of the new president ought to be.

CHAPTER 28

Earlier in the week I had tried to ride my motorcycle into southern Lebanon along the coast. Just before Sidon, the road funnelled into a military checkpoint complete with looping razor wire, steel blockade jacks, and a red-and-white guardhouse. A soldier motioned for me to shut off the engine.

"I'm sorry," he said. "Motorcycles are not allowed south of here."

"Why not?"

"These are the new rules," he said. "You must return to Beirut. Or put your motorcycle in a truck."

"So I can go to Sidon, just not on a motorcycle."

"That's right."

"And I can even take my bike into Sidon if I use a truck."

"Yes."

"That's ridiculous," I said. "Why can't I just ride in?"

"New rules," he said. He showed me where I could turn around.

"But, I really want to see southern Lebanon," I pleaded.

"You want to see southern Lebanon?" he said. "Try Google Earth."

With that, I returned to Beirut.

Days later, I rented a car with my friend Sean. In just the right light, you could make out a moustache and goatee on Sean, but they seldom showed up in photographs. He had thick, rimless glasses. He wore a toque a lot. Here in the Middle East, like others in his position, Sean battled the misconceptions of a society intolerant of multiculturalism. He got labelled.

"Yeah, it's frustrating sometimes," he said. "Just because I look Chinese, people assume I'm from China. I mean, I was born and raised in Vancouver. I have a perfectly clean Canadian accent. Still, they think that I'm from Asia."

Quite right. Though I stopped nodding when he mentioned the clean accent; I could have sworn that he said, "Still, dey tink dat I'm from Asia."

Anyway, I liked having Sean around to explain things for me. As far as I know, he was the only person I hung out with who had actually read a book by Robert Fisk. Compared to me, that made him a respectable authority on Lebanese politics. We spent hours one day over coffee as he broke down the current political situation. When he finished, I reviewed my notes from the conversation. I must have looked confused.

"OK, look. It all comes down to this," he said. I picked up my pen. "Lebanon is fucked."

While I finished up paperwork for the car, Sean left to get passport photos. I had mine already. We needed them to apply for permission papers at a military base in Sidon to travel in the south.

Sean and I rolled up to the base precisely at 2:00 p.m., closing time for the office. We confirmed, at least, that this was the right place, and that they would open again tomorrow to issue our papers. Dejected, we drove straight to the nearest McDonald's.

"This is the equivalent of chicks having chocolate after getting dumped," said Sean.

Sidon is one of Lebanon's largest centres, behind Beirut and Tripoli. It's old. The warm waters of the Mediterranean have lapped against the shores of Sidon for thousands of years. Once a prominent shipping hub, it was further renowned for timber cutters who worked the cedars of Lebanon, and for its skilled craftsmen.

When early religious texts refer to Sidon they often mention its sister city, Tyre, as well, along with a horrible list of things that God wanted to do to them. Through the ages, Sidon has hosted several prominent visitors, including the Prophet Elijah and Saint Paul. Even Jesus made the journey north to Tyre and Sidon, where he acted strangely put-offish towards a local woman who needed help.

Today, Sidon boasts a small crusader castle that seems to rise up from the water. It has a fine souk and several museums.

Yes, Sidon has a lot to offer, but Sean and I wanted to see a landmark of another kind, one that I had read about in a local newspaper. I couldn't find any information about it on my tourist map, however. Even Sean's guidebook omitted the feature except for one indirect reference that warned against swimming anywhere near the city, no matter how appealing the water might look. It neglected to mention why.

We didn't have to travel far to find out. From where we parked the car, we could still see the Golden Arches of McDonald's. As we turned towards the sea, there towered before us a twenty-metre high mountain of garbage.

Rubbish Mountain is an environmental catastrophe, a growing pile of household and industrial waste perched on the edge of the Mediterranean. In fact, it slopes into the sea. The same waters that have splashed Sidon's rocky coast for millennia now erode the very foundation that supports tons of untreated waste. Plastic bags and bottles, car tires, rotting animal carcasses and chemical refuse routinely slough into the water, killing marine life and damaging the nets of local fishermen. One of the worst incidents saw an estimated 150 tons of debris fracture off into the water, where currents carried it to foreign shores.

Not everyone viewed the avalanche in a negative light.

Some Palestinian refugees, restricted from working proper jobs, earn their living on the mountain, scavenging for aluminum or cardboard – anything to sell for a few dollars. To them, the avalanche exposed a new field for exploration.

Sean and I grabbed our cameras. In order to bypass any security that might not welcome our presence, we climbed over a cinderblock fence. Walking along the water's edge towards the refuse pile, we each processed the view in our own way.

"That's a mountain of garbage!" Sean exclaimed. "It's a mountain of garbage right on the ocean!"

The sight stunned me. Speechless, I raised my camera, zoomed in and pressed the shutter release. I composed another shot. In the bottom left corner of the frame, right by the sea, I noticed a tent dwarfed by the garbage. Several people stood there, most likely Palestinian refugees, and half a dozen others stood on the summit, filtering through the trash.

The people looked up as we drew closer. One of the men raised his hand and shouted, and then several of them began walking towards us.

"I'm really not sure if we should be here," I said as I snapped another picture. "And I'm pretty certain we shouldn't be taking pictures. I don't imagine the government is keen to advertise this place."

With that, we returned to the car.

On our way back to Beirut, we drove up a winding road to a village nestled in the Chouf Mountains. From a roadside vantage point, we looked out over stone houses. The sun slipped behind forested hills into the sea. I imagined a group of Palestinians standing atop Rubbish Mountain, not far away. They turned to watch the sunset, too. From that height, right next to the water, it must be beautiful.

CHAPTER 29

I poked at the neutral sensor below the shift lever until the green light flickered on. The engine didn't want to start at first, but it finally sputtered to life. After that it rose in pitch to a healthy idle. The exhaust came in metered bursts, making the leaves jump on a nearby bush. In the cool air you could see the smoke. Sometimes the Oscillator puffed out a smoke ring just for fun. As the bike warmed up, I looked it over.

"I know I've been ignoring you," I whispered, patting the gas tank, "and I'm sorry." I strapped up my helmet, still talking softly to the machine. "It's just that I haven't left Beirut much these past few weeks, and when I did I had company. You know. It's easier to take a taxi."

If the Oscillator resented the neglect, it didn't show. Together we rode north, in the direction of Tripoli. Nearing the city, I turned away from the coast and climbed into the hills towards a low bank of cloud. When I stopped at the edge of a town to check my map, an old man waved me over to join him for coffee on his porch. Bundled up against a chill in the mountain air, he wore a long woollen jacket and a black hat. We took turns leafing through my Arabic phrasebook in an effort to communicate, but that only frustrated us both. In the end we sat quietly, enjoying the cool air and hot coffee.

One side of the man's porch nudged the road, while the other side opened onto a rocky yard. From there, the property dropped into the holy ground of the Qadisha Valley. The valley is home to several Christian monasteries and the town of Bcharre, an important centre for the Christian Maronites and their right-wing Phalange Party – the people who carried out the Shatila massacres.

Crags in this valley often split open into caves, and these caves have for centuries attracted hermits aspiring to religious perfection. Whether any have attained it or not, who can say? Still, you have to admire their resolve. At least these guys follow beliefs through to their logical conclusion. ("Wait. You mean, after living for maybe ninety years we die, but not really? We go on living in heaven for billions and billions and billions of years and then billions more forever and ever? Fuck it. I'm going to wait in a cave.")

Looking across the gap, I could see a clutch of white houses perched at the far edge of grey cliffs. The cliffs were all mottled with ochre and rust. Hardy shrubs with green leaves clung to the rock, while farther upslope the leaves had gone yellow. Higher still, a dusting of snow settled on grey mountaintops.

Way down below, the Qadisha River ran through the valley. Its headwaters are in a grotto very near the Cedars of God. That was my destination, the last remaining grove of Lebanon's ancient cedars.

I stood to leave, thanking the man for his kindness. I gestured towards the view. The man smiled.

The road wound through villages with red roofs and Christian symbols, through Bcharre, past a domed church with two towers, and farther up to the cedars. Parking the bike, I slid out of the saddle to stand on numb feet. I swung my arms to warm the blood in my fingers. As my joints had grown stiff from the cold, I took several testing steps before picking up the pace. Walking down, I passed through an opening in a stone fence and entered the forest. Technically it was closed for the season, but that only meant that I had the place all to myself.

My footsteps made no sound: the path lay beneath a blanket of needles and seed cones that had fallen from the trees. Patches of snow gathered in shady hollows. Each tree was anchored to the earth with a wide base, its thick boughs stretched out like giants flexing for show.

A cold rain fell as I padded along. It washed the scent of cedar right out of the air. Water trickled off my head along ringlets of hair, pausing at the tips before dropping away in front of my eyes.

I looked around for a sign of life. I listened. Nothing but the plunking of rain off my shoulders. I wished that I could share the moment with someone. A few times I even caught myself speaking out loud – was I talking to the trees or just to myself? Either way, if the trees heard me they remained silent … just like God. Of course he was there, too, if he was anywhere at all.

My Christian Ethics teacher in high school said that God was everywhere at all times. In fact, God so permeated everything that he even existed in the space between atoms. He was with us when we were still embryos and he stitched us together there.

Once I considered that, I began to chase the high alt con-clusion like the hermits in the valley. God exists between atoms? Then he lives between the nails of a suicide bomb-er's vest. He's in the semen of a rapist and the bloody tissue beneath the fingernails of his victim. How can that God be good? There's another assumption.

Usually when people say God is good, they really mean "God is good to me at this moment." Because somewhere, right now, there's a man abusing his teenaged daughter and

God is in that room too. He's listening to her scream. And he's watching her kill herself when it's over. And he's sending her to hell. But God is good because we prayed and the sun came out for our church picnic.

Suddenly I didn't mind being all alone, walking quietly on the soft path. God might have been right there with me, and everywhere else, too. And he might be good. If you want it bad enough, there are explanations for everything.

Returning to the bike, I wiped the seat with the back of my glove to clear away the water. The map showed a track that crossed over the mountains before dropping down into the Beqaa Valley. I looked up into the hills. Heavy fog had settled over the peaks, making it impossible to see. On the map, though, the route looked appealing.

I idled up to the only tourist shop still open this late in the season. I asked the girl behind the counter about the path. Was it open? Is it a good road?

The girl was unaccustomed to fielding questions like this in English. She could really only talk about the price of her curios. After searching for the words, she did manage to articulate a warning. "There is snow," she said. "It's too difficult for him." She meant the Oscillator. "He'll fall."

I decided to ride up anyway and take a look for myself. I've ridden in the snow before and I was imagining the dry, powdery stuff I had seen lower in the valley.

With a wave to the girl, I rode into the fog. I'll bet she could still hear my engine when heavy snow forced me to turn around. As the road pushed through the clouds, it entered a landscape of slush. I pressed on, though, thinking that I might be near the crest of the pass. But the sleet that stuck to my visor provided no traction for my tires. The Oscillator very nearly did fall. When I stopped in the middle of the road to warm my hands, I couldn't get moving again. The back tire just spun and spun. Defeated, I executed a fifteen-point turn-around to retreat. Dragging both feet, I slipped back down the mountain until the sleet became cold rain once again. As I rode past the tourist shop I looked for the girl. She was gone.

When I had left Beirut that morning, I had brought along a small backpack with the intention of staying in a new town for the night, but now, too tired and wet to bother finding a hostel, I settled in for a miserable ride in the dark and rain all the way back to Beirut.

CHAPTER 30

Pulling the blankets up to my chin, I lay awake listening to the storm from the comfort of a familiar bed. I smiled. Wind rattled my window. Rain pinged off the tin flashing of the roof above.

In the morning, I could see blue sky. I had mixed feelings about that. It meant that I could stick to my plan of leaving Lebanon, but part of me wanted an excuse to stay. With heavy weather, I could have justified another week in Beirut. They still hadn't chosen a president in Lebanon, and more elections were on the way.

Packing up took a long time. Just three weeks in one location and I had forgotten where everything belonged. After sorting it all out, I shuttled my bags downstairs.

Zaher gave me a hand-drawn map that he claimed would lead straight to Damascus. Following it, I found a twisty road that lifted me out of the city to the top of a mountain pass before descending past military posts and tanks covered with camouflage netting. Down in the valley, I kept the sun on my right until I reached the border. A quick exit from Lebanon saw me in an expanse of no man's land that stretched for kilometres. I kept motoring until I arrived at the Syrian gates.

Approaching Damascus, I followed a wide street to Umayyad Square, a busy traffic circle that connects several major roadways. It had a large fountain in the middle. On its edge there was a sword-like sculpture made of concrete and stained glass. The circle was ringed with manicured green spaces and buildings such as the Damascus Opera House, a state-run television station, and the luxurious Sheraton Hotel. Years later this square would become the scene of pro-government rallies that would draw thousands of demonstrators, but for now it was just an orderly traffic circle.

Given my poor track record of navigation in the city, I only relaxed the grip on my bars when I spotted a distinct high-rise building. It was an abandoned shell of a building, actually. From what I had heard, the engineers had only discovered a dangerously unstable foundation beneath the structure after workers had nearly finished construction. Now it served as a convenient landmark to help tourists find their hostels.

I went to bed early that night because I had a date with the Iranian embassy in the morning. That's really why I left Beirut: my Iranian visa went through. I should say that my visa went through *apparently*. I was keeping my enthusiasm in check because I didn't trust Mahmoud.

Ever since leaving Istanbul, I had dedicated my spare time to irritating Mahmoud of the Incompetent Visa Agency. I never expected anything to come of it, you understand: I just sort of picked it up as a hobby. I plugged up his voicemail with angry messages. I sent e-mails. Also, I posted about the agency on popular travel forums. I wrote about how they had lied, how they had ruined my trip and taken my money. I sent Mahmoud links to those blogs.

As it turned out, all that badgering annoyed him exactly as much as I hoped it would. When he responded to my e-mail at last, I could tell that he had done so with clenched teeth. In a curt letter he wrote that I should pick up my visa in Damascus. It would be there, he promised.

Of course, I doubted that very much. What made it seem especially unlikely is that Iran had just kicked out the Canadian ambassador again. However, as I had to leave Beirut sooner or later, and as my route led through Damascus anyway, I decided to investigate further.

Getting out of the taxi at the Iranian embassy in the morning, it amused me to see the Canadian embassy right next door. That must make for an awkward block party. I wondered if employees at the two buildings ever acknowledged each other as they showed up for work.

"Morning, Gord."

"Morning, Mohammed."

Probably not.

A man behind the window took my passport and disappeared to look for the authorization number. When he returned, he gave me two identical forms. The papers called for information about my family and profession.

I started filling them out, but when I came to a blank space marked "Religion," I stopped. My pen hovered over the field for a second or two. What were they looking for? Never mind that. What could I honestly write? Without touching the paper, I traced an answer through the air with my pen: None.

My stomach rolled over and I felt tightness in my chest. That answer didn't feel right. What had I said to Chikako in Istanbul? She had asked if I was Christian and I'd said yes. I said yes, but then I blathered on to explain what I meant. I didn't know anything, I said. I could be wrong. I just hoped. Even then, my hope extended only to a distilled Christian faith, to what I believed to be its essence – forgiveness through Jesus. I looked at the small space on the form: Religion. It was not an essay question.

I traced another answer through the air: Skeptic. That's not a religion. A theocratic nation would not accept that answer, anyway, but was it true? I am skeptical, yes, but it's hard. It's hard filtering through a religious book for sufficient revelation while dismissing other parts as allegory. How do you differentiate? Some say that if you want part of the Bible, you must take it all. The Bible is God-breathed, they say, and is therefore perfect. (Usually those same people believe that man is God-breathed, but that he is fallen and horribly flawed.)

Anyway, to take the Bible literally means accepting a talking donkey. It means that a fortified city fell to a trumpet blast and that time stood still while Joshua tidied up a bit of ethnic cleansing. It means that God told Abraham to kill his child, but that child sacrifice never entered God's mind. It means the writing on the wall, surviving a burning furnace, three days inside a fish, virgin birth, walking on water. Some of it gets pretty hard to swallow. Yeah, but if God wrote the laws of the universe, then all of these things are possible. Everything is.

Once, while having this same discussion back in Canada, a friend observed, "Just because something seems crazy, doesn't mean that it's not true." Quite right. At one time it seemed daft to believe that the Earth was round. Except that statement can be used as a defence for every single faith and for every crazy idea.

Imagine if that same friend rushed up to me, breathless, and said, "This morning, in perfect eighteenth-century English, my cat told me to stop masturbating!" Well, if I took the Bible literally then I'd have to admit that, OK, that's possible. But I wouldn't do that. Instead, I would tell my friend to see a psychiatrist and to get a new cat. What would you do?

And why are some of us less dismissive of strange historical accounts? Perhaps God's interaction with us as a species has changed, you say. Humans have evolved. In our infancy, maybe God stepped into our stories more often. He spoke through a donkey, a disembodied hand, a burning bush, or prophets. As we added pages to history books, God may have let us go, just as a father should do when his son becomes a man. Maybe he speaks subtly now. Possibly, for the moment, he doesn't speak at all because he already said every necessary thing.

A more elegant solution is to conclude that religious texts contain metaphors. Maybe it's just like Reza Aslan says in *No god but God:* "To ask whether Moses actually parted the Red Sea, or whether Jesus truly raised Lazarus from the dead, or whether the word of God indeed poured through the lips of Muhammad, is to ask irrelevant questions. The only question that matters with regard to a religion and its mythology is 'What do these stories mean?'" Careful not to throw out the baby with the bathwater, I guess.

I looked up at the man behind the window, who was frowning at me. These forms shouldn't take so long.

In the air above the religion field, I traced another answer: Working it out with fear and trembling. That's not a religion, either. Anyway, it wouldn't fit in the box. Putting pen to paper at last, I wrote "Christian" in neat, blocky letters. Because I'm from the West, it's the answer that the window man would expect. I had made too big a deal of it, I know. So, I wrote "Christian" and I left it there. In the air behind my answer I added, "but it's not my fault."

Once I handed in all my paperwork, the man slipped me a piece of paper with instructions to return later and collect my passport. I stepped outside. A taxi had taken me to the embassy, but I decided to walk back. After zipping up my jacket, I shaded my eyes to look down the street. I could just make out the abandoned shell of a high-rise building near my hostel, off in the distance.

What a waste, I thought. *People should examine their foundations more carefully before building a tower.*

CHAPTER 31

When I picked up my passport later that day, I leafed through it, looking for the visa. It was there, a sticker covering an entire page. I ran my fingers over the silver embossed design of Iran in the corner. At the top it read, "Visa Islamic Republic of Iran." Almost everything else was written in Farsi. They had not given me as much time as I wanted, but it would get me into Persia.

I thought about the maps and the Farsi phrasebook that I had sent home – and the Iranian guidebook. The traveller's bible. How short-sighted of me to have thrown it away the moment it seemed irrelevant. I could sure use it now that I had my visa.

Or maybe not. Yes, I had my visa, but I still had decisions to make. A journey to Iran meant backtracking thousands of kilometres through Syria and Turkey. On that northeasterly ride, the characteristics of a cruel winter would grow more pronounced with virtually every rotation of my wheels. Once at the border, if I managed to get there, I would face a high mountain road that passed through the shadow of Mount Ararat in Turkey before snaking through the Zagros Mountains in Iran. As these mountains endure blizzards beginning in November, they would have provided ample suffering for me even way back when I intended to cross. Now, in the middle of December, the pass would be plugged with snow. It would be even more formidable than the one that turned me around in Lebanon.

Maybe if I found a place to store the bike, I could leave it in Syria while I took a side trip to Iran. Although that would be much easier said than done. When I entered Syria, my passport got stamped to say that I brought a vehicle. If I tried to leave without the bike, I might forfeit the deposit on the carnet. Besides, this was supposed to be a motorcycle trip. The whole point was to get my bike into Iran, wasn't it?

No matter how I looked at it, I could not see a reasonable solution. The smart play here would be to initiate the return journey. Back at the hostel, I lay a heavy head down on the pillow and immediately fell asleep.

A knock on the door jolted me awake. Rubbing my eyes, I got up to answer the door.

"Hey, man, good to see you," said Steve. "Let's get something to eat."

This was unexpected. I had met Steve in Lebanon. He left the day after I arrived, but on my very first night in Beirut, he guided me through Tent City and along the Corniche.

I grabbed my jacket. Steve showed me to a restaurant where, for less than a dollar, we each ordered a bowl of *ful*, a traditional peasant meal of fava beans mashed together with olive oil. It came with a tray of pickles, beets and onions. We ate everything with our hands, scooping up the *ful* with pieces of flatbread. After supper, we ordered a narghile and sat outside smoking.

A group of young Syrian men walked by on the street. They all stared at Steve. "Jackie Chan!" they laughed.

"See what I mean?" said Steve. Steve complained that he got pigeonholed in the Middle East, too, just like Sean in Beirut. With his long hair he reminded people of Jackie

Chan from *Shanghai Noon*, although Steve was of Japanese descent, born and raised in the United States.

"Sometimes they walk up to me and go 'Chin, ching, chong.' That's when I snap," he said. "I get right up in their face and challenge them to fight. It really freaks them out, too. I don't think they see a lot of confrontational people who look Asian."

A cold wind lifted embers from the pipe while at the same time crushing smoke rings before they even left my lips. I zipped up my jacket as far as it would go and pulled my toque down to cover my ears. Steve cradled his cup of tea, hunching his shoulders and drawing his elbows in to his side. It was dark by the time we finished our pipes, but still early.

Perhaps the chill in the air pushed us that way, but we soon found ourselves at the door of Hammam Nureddin, the oldest public bath in Damascus. I had been there once already, during my short layover before Lebanon.

On that first visit I went alone. I didn't know what to expect, so I paid for the complete package. A man behind the counter gave me three coloured elastics to wear on my wrist, each one representing a different service.

A few stairs led to a carpeted dressing area overlooking a room with an ornamental fountain. I climbed onto a high bench along the wall with a little jump, and sat there swinging my feet.

This hammam catered exclusively to men. There was no need for separate change rooms, but full nudity was forbidden. When I had layered down to my underwear, an employee came over with a thin towel. Turning his head, he spread it out for me like a privacy curtain, wrapping it around my waist when I was naked.

I followed him down onto a marble floor next to the fountain. There he gave me a pair of high-heeled wooden sandals that were designed, as far as I could tell, to undermine the wearer's sense of masculine identity. With their low coefficient of friction on wet marble, the shoes reduced my gait to a series of perky steps, hands held out for balance. Even then, I skated about like Bambi on ice. Of course, Bambi didn't have a towel around his knees. With every slip, the fabric snapped taut like the skin on a tambourine while, at the same time, the knot at my waist loosened off in subtle increments.

Still in the public dressing room, the towel initiated a slow descent. There was nothing I could do about it. My hands were full of accoutrements for various stages of the bath. In an effort to keep the towel from dropping away, I assumed a semi-squatting position. Fixing my hips in place, I proceeded with alternating pivots, first on my left, then on my right foot.

This got me to the sauna. I kept squatting until the door closed, and then I adjusted my towel. Beads of perspiration grew on my skin as I took stock of the accessories. I had with me a bar of soap, a silver bowl, and what looked like a roll of shredded wheat. The soap made sense, but I would have to figure everything else out later.

When I had finished the sauna, a boy led me into the general wash area. A heavy wooden door opened onto a room that echoed with the sound of voices and running water. From one corner, steam hissed out of a small doorway to form a thick cloud. Standing, I could only make out shadowy figures. When I bowed low beneath the steam, I could see men sitting or lying on the marble floor. They lounged along the walls next to basins overflowing with clear water. Each basin had two silver taps pouring into it, one of nearly scalding water and the other ice cold. The mixture in the basin was pleasantly warm.

I sat down on the floor next to my own basin. Still unsure of what to do, I watched the other men. Like me, each of them had a silver bowl. With that, they scooped water from the basin to douse themselves. The men lathered up with soap, using the shredded wheat as a sort of washcloth. They also scrubbed each other, rather affectionately, I thought. Lathering, scrubbing, rinsing, repeating. I got it.

When I could lather and rinse myself no more, I decided to redeem another elastic to get my abrasive.

What's an "abrasive," anyway? I wondered.

I pulled open the heavy door and picked my way into a side room. There I found a fat man covered in body hair with just a small towel to create a shadow of mystery. We locked eyes. I spun to leave, but I couldn't move fast enough in my slippery shoes.

"Sit!" the man shouted. He sat me roughly down on the wet floor where he proceeded to scrub the shit out of me with a Scotch-Brite pad.

"Ah, wow, that's rough," I said, or something to that effect. "Ha, ha. Easy there. Let's not…"

"Down!" he yelled. I lay down on my stomach.

"Turn!" I turned.

In this way, the man stripped away most of my epidermis, along with my dignity.

"Finished!" he said at last. Stinging from the experience, I slipped away in effeminate sandals to the massage room. I hopped onto the table, where I sat whimpering. Moments later, another mostly naked man pounded me down like he was tenderizing a beefsteak. He even cracked my back and neck. With my face buried in the pillow I tried to remember if I had seen a chiropractic diploma on the wall.

By the time the massage man let me go, I had stopped

looking people in the eye. I was led once more to the basin room, where I was told that I could linger as long as I liked.

Instead, I returned to the dressing room with the high benches. An attendant towelled me dry, wrapped me in fresh towels, and ran off to fetch tea and ice water. So that was my first experience with a hammam. I decided then that I would never go through that ordeal again. If I ever did go back I would only pay for the sauna and skip everything else.

Steve looked around as we stepped up to the counter. "I've never been to a hammam," he said.

"Oh, right," I said. "In that case, I recommend you get the complete package."

CHAPTER 32

After obtaining my Iranian visa, I spent many fitful nights struggling with my options. During the day I paced the hotel or took walks in the old city, searching my brain for an affordable solution to get the Oscillator and me into Iran.

Finally, I decided to throw in the towel once again, sticking to my original decision. I would ride south, into Jordan, and then Israel, perhaps. I packed my bags to leave the next day.

In the morning I awoke to a frigid rain. Leaving Damascus could wait. I crawled back into bed, where I spent most of the day writing on my computer and watching DVDs – anything to keep from second-guessing myself.

Come nightfall, all the thoughts I had suppressed sprang to life. I tossed and turned in bed. I kicked my blankets onto the floor, punched my pillow, and pulled the blankets back onto the bed. My eyelids quivered as I squeezed them shut, while behind them my mind projected quick movies of every possible scenario for the trip ahead. They all ended with regret.

Forcing myself to breathe slow, I lay on my back, staring at the ceiling. Eventually I fell asleep, but only after resolving to dedicate at least one more day to Iran. If I had known what that decision would cost me in time and effort, I would have lain awake all night.

CHAPTER 33

I explained my situation to a travel agent with short grey hair that wrapped around the side of his head from ear to ear.

"This should be easy," he said. "Maybe you can leave the bike with a customs garage and fly." He went on to explain that I first needed to go to the Immigration office to get another Syrian visa before he could sell me a round-trip flight. He agreed to go with me to translate.

We walked across the street to the office, where we found a mass of people packed into a small room. The travel agent placed a cigarette between his lips and, squinting against the smoke, he pushed his way through the crowd. We bumped up against a heavy wooden desk cluttered with paper. The man seated there wore a drab uniform with black shoulder boards. After examining my passport, he shook his head and sent us away.

"He said you cannot leave Syria without your moto," the agent explained. Of course, I already knew that. Going on, he said, "There is no customs garage, either. But I think you can still do it. You can leave your motorcycle at the border with Lebanon."

His plan went like this: I would ride to the border, clear the motorcycle through customs, and leave Syria. Before riding into Lebanon, I would stash the bike in no man's land between countries. Then I would turn around and enter

Syria again with a clean visa, one that made no mention of a vehicle.

The plan was wacky and I tried it, but even after several rewrites I haven't found a way to make it interesting. In summary, I stamped out of Syria. I went to a Dunkin' Donuts situated between borders. I re-entered Syria with some difficulty (they didn't believe that I just wanted a donut), and I returned to Damascus with the motorcycle.

I would have been right back where I started, but somewhere along the way I had picked up a letter from an important official that explained everything to his friend in Immigration. I was told to show up at the Immigration office at 8:00 p.m. with the letter and with a Syrian friend who would take charge of the motorcycle in my absence.

When I got back to the hostel around mid-afternoon, I set out to find a Syrian guarantor. Unfortunately, everyone I approached refused to help. It was, after all, a rather large favour to ask.

With some time to kill before my meeting, I gathered all my documents and stepped outside. Really, I just wanted to lie down, but if I stopped moving I might slip into a coma.

Arriving at the Immigration office later that night, I passed through a dark doorway. I scuffed up a flight of stairs and plopped myself onto a vinyl chair in the hallway to wait. It was a busy hallway, but in quiet moments I could hear the hum of an overhead fluorescent light. It seemed odd to see such a rush of people in a government office at this late hour, but I didn't really think about it.

With my elbows propped up on my knees, I rested my head in my hands and stared at the floor. The white tiles had dark inlays of stone. One reminded me of a slab of bacon, another of something you might see under a microscope – a cancerous tumour, for example. That would only make sense, with all the cigarette smoke in the air. Even the walls had the colour of a spent cigarette filter, but I think someone had painted them that way on purpose. I tugged at the front of my shirt to move some air over my body, now dripping with sweat.

I wiped away the perspiration from my eyes with the heel of my hands, and then looked up. Desperate Arabs, each one searching for the correct sequence of rubber stamps and signatures, shoved past one another on their way from one crowded room to the next. The men wore long-sleeved dress shirts stained with sweat, and the women wore black chadors. They fanned themselves with passports. The rooms had windows, but they remained closed.

At precisely eight o'clock, I stood up and unfolded my note. I showed it to someone who pointed me up another flight of stairs, where I found two rooms. In one, a haggard man and his desk sat like an island in a sea of people. It would take forever to reach him. The other room was quiet. It contained a few Syrian flags and one sizeable desk with an expensive leather chair. A framed picture of Bashar al-Assad hung on the wall behind the desk, and in front of that stood a distinguished-looking man in uniform. He had a cell phone pressed to his ear.

The man snatched the note from my hand and read it without ever looking at me or putting the phone down. Then he pushed a button on his desk – the kind of button that usually opens a trap door in the movies. Thankfully, this one only triggered a chime in another room. A boy hurried in. The man barked orders at him and dismissed us both.

For the next hour, the kid hustled me through hot rooms packed with tired people clutching passports. Finally he left me with an official in a back room who sat there, leafing through my paperwork.

"You wait!" he snapped. Then he pushed my papers to the very edge of his desk where they sat, teetering on the brink.

I settled into my chair. Suddenly travel-weary, I longed for home. *I should go back,* I thought. I was running out of money. All this effort to get into Iran was just for show. To be honest, I was just going through the motions now so that when I failed – and I would fail – at least I could tell everyone that I tried.

With no energy left for optimism, my thoughts spiralled downward. I nearly stood to leave when an old woman looked at me and smiled. She was short and chubby, wrapped in a chador with only her face showing through. That woman smiled at me, nodding encouragement. I smiled back. It was the first time that I had noticed an individual in the crowd. Then I looked down at the passports in her hand and my smile wilted.

Shocked to attention, I saw the crowd in a different light. They all carried the same type of passport – green ones with gold writing on the cover. A proud eagle stood in the middle with Arabic script above his head. Below him, in English, was written: "Republic of Iraq."

These people were all refugees, all of them fleeing the destruction, death, and despair that had settled over their homeland. And these people here in Syria were the lucky ones. Suddenly my little motorcycle vacation didn't seem important. I didn't feel so discouraged, either. Like the smile on my face, my self-pity faded, too ... at least for a while.

Understanding the context of all that humanity pressed together in a hot building increased my tolerance for bureaucracy. With just one smile from an old woman, I felt as though I could now sit in that office for weeks without complaint.

Fortunately, it never came to that. The boy who led me

there returned with a note from the distinguished man upstairs. He pushed it across the desk at the official who had snapped at me. There followed a pronounced silence as the man read it, then a brief discussion among the workers.

Several Iraqis turned to smile at me. One of them interpreted what the officials were saying.

"It's OK," he said. "It will work for you now. It's easy here. It's all about important people."

The angry official, who was not so angry anymore, looked up and said, "You need a letter from your hotel saying that you are staying there. The boy will go with you to translate."

Together, my runner and I hurried out of the building. High up in the dark hills, I could see a row of open-air restaurants that overlooked the city. They appeared as a crisp line of coloured lights that ran diagonally up from left to right. Just for a moment I closed my eyes and smiled, breathing deeply of the clean air. A cool breeze kissed my face as we hurried along the sidewalk beside a small park with fountains, shrubs, and little white bridges. We passed a drinking fountain on the street, inscribed in Arabic and English that read, "Always remember God," before trotting up the metal stairs of a pedestrian overpass and moving towards the abandoned tower that marked my hotel.

For the first time in weeks, I felt as if I might succeed in getting to Iran. I still had no guarantor, but it seemed as if I had bypassed that step somehow.

Bursting through the door at the hotel, I found my favourite employee on duty. I never caught his real name, but we all called him Harley. (I learned, years later on another visit, that his name was Halid and that I was just mispronouncing it.)

Harley was young, no more than twenty, I guessed. He had black hair greased back and a baby face. A dark suit jacket hung about his frame much as it would have from a coat hanger.

I explained that I needed a letter from the hotel, but my runner demanded that he return with us to the Immigration office. Harley grabbed his identification card and together we rushed back into the night. As we trotted along I tried to gauge the vibe from Harley. If he was upset, he hid it well. I wanted to ask whether he would get into trouble if for some reason I could not return for my bike, but I kept my mouth shut.

Back into the heat and stale air, we pushed through the crowd once again. Harley presented his ID. He signed some papers and then I got a letter covered with stamps and signatures.

That was it.

As we stepped outside, I looked at my watch. It was half past nine, but the lights were on at the travel office. The agent who tried to help me over ten hours ago was still there, too. I showed him my letter and asked him to check flights for me. I would return in the morning to book it.

CHAPTER 34

Forty-eight hours later, I boarded a Syrian Air flight bound for Tehran. My back ached and my right leg tingled like it was connected to a battery tender, but I was happy. Unable to sleep, I stared into a black window as the jet arced north over Turkey to avoid Iraqi airspace.

The past two days had been stressful, but productive. After booking my flight, I found a bank machine to withdraw the maximum allowable amount of American dollars. I did this once again on the day of my flight. Where foreigners are concerned, Iran is a cash society. Neither my bank nor credit cards would be of any use once I got off the plane.

With the help of three other motorcycle travellers, I rolled the Oscillator into the back courtyard of the hotel. We pushed it through the front door, up marble stairs, past reception and into the common area before squeezing it down a narrow hall. It took all four of us to move a metal cabinet out of the way. Then we removed a wooden door from its hinges in order to back the bike through a small kitchen, finally wiggling it through another door and out into the rear courtyard where I would lock it up. In my mind, the bike had never been more secure.

A friend had given me his tattered guidebook to the Middle East before leaving Beirut, and I opened it now. Iran is the world's only Shia Islamic state, it said, although some have argued that parts of Lebanon under Hezbollah control would also fit that description. The split between Sunni and Shia Islam happened early in the Muslim story, just a few decades after the Prophet Mohammed died, but the groundwork for the bloody fracture was laid even before his death.

It's a long and tragic story that boils down to the question of who should have succeeded the Prophet. Who should have led that small group of people who recognized Mohammed as the Prophet of God?

If Mohammed had had sons, that question might have answered itself, but he didn't. He had daughters and grandsons. And he had a trusted cousin and son-in-law named Ali, who lived in constant friction with Mohammed's favourite and youngest wife, the childless Aisha.

In *After the Prophet*, Lesley Hazleton paints a chilling picture of the wars and assassinations that plagued the Muslim community in the early years, when they struggled to find a new leader. After reading it, I'm sympathetic to the long-suffering Ali and, therefore, to the Shia who claim him as a legitimate leader. I'm sure other books would make a compelling case for the Sunnis. At any rate, it was Mohammed's cousin the fourth caliph, Ali, and his successors who have shaped the minority Shia into the group they are today.

Touching down in Tehran at midnight, I stepped off the plane into the Imam Khomeini International Airport, a bright building with glass walls, silver cables and a blue ceiling. Breezing through customs, I found myself in the cold night air searching for a taxi.

With only three weeks on my visa, I needed to make the most of my time. I considered heading south to one of the cities I had circled on the map, but it would take all night to get there. Already my eyes burned for sleep, and my body shook from fatigue. I needed the closest bed.

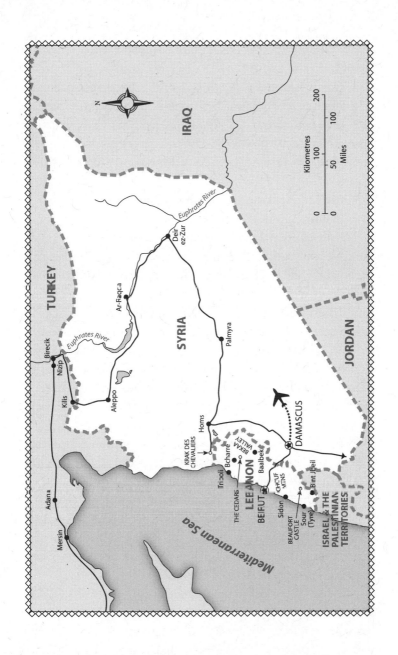

Climbing into the taxi, I placed a small backpack on the floor by my feet.

"Imam Khomeini Square," I said. The driver nodded. He spun the wheel towards Tehran and stepped on the gas. The road was embedded with coloured lights, giving it the appearance of a runway. Maybe the driver got that impression, too, because he seemed to be building up speed for takeoff.

"Majeed," said the driver, tapping his chest.

"Jeremy," I said. We shook hands.

Majeed offered me tea from his thermos. Beyond small talk, we could not really communicate. Majeed spoke very little English, and the Farsi phrasebook I had purchased for the trip now sat in a box in my parents' house in Saskatchewan. Regardless, Majeed had something important to say.

"Before 1979," he fumbled, "Iran OK. Alcohol, OK. Now ... no OK." In this manner, he went on to decry the age of ayatollahs and the current establishment. Majeed looked at least ten years older than me. He could have been in high school during the Iranian Revolution. What a horrible time to have endured restrictions on alcohol and immodesty.

This driver was the first person I met in Iran, but in the weeks to come I would encounter many others who complained about their government and all the restrictions inherent within the Islamic Republic. In some ways, the riots that followed the 2009 presidential elections were predictable. And it doesn't take a genius to see that more riots are in Iran's future. You just can't clamp down on people like that and not expect some sort of backlash.

Judging by most people I met during my visit, I'd say that the youth want governmental reform, but that's only my narrow opinion. Obviously I didn't conduct a proper survey. The people who were most likely to feel comfortable speaking with me, a Westerner, would also be the ones already predisposed towards changing the system.

Majeed and I raced through the empty streets of Tehran, a sprawling city of 14 million people with rows of concrete buildings. The lights overhead looked like childish drawings of flying birds, wilting V's that reflected soft light from below. Electric palm trees glowed orange, green, and red, while artificial fireworks on sticks exploded silently. The ayatollahs may have outlawed dancing and booze, but for whatever reason they had chosen to keep the disco lights.

As we careened through the sleeping city, another cab driver caught us up and convinced Majeed to stop the car. The drivers parked side by side in the middle of the road to chat.

They spoke Farsi, but I could follow the conversation by their intonation. The other driver had nearly run out of fuel. Benzene, as they called it, was a rationed commodity in Iran. Each driver had a fuel card that allowed them to purchase so many litres per month and no more. This driver had used up all of his credits, and he wanted to buy Majeed's card.

"Of course. No problem," said Majeed. He gave a chuckle as if the other driver had made a big deal out of nothing. "Take my card, friend. What is a little benzene between brothers?" Majeed even refused to accept payment, waving the other driver away with a smile and, I imagined, a playful admonishment, "Just keep a weather eye on your fuel gauge! Ha, ha."

Majeed smiled at me, shaking his head as we continued on our way. "Some people," he seemed to say. We drove in silence for a long time after that and I finally leaned my head against the window to sleep. Then Majeed screamed. Bracing myself against the dashboard, I prepared for the worst. When nothing happened, I turned to look at Majeed. Still driving along dark streets, we stared at each other now in wide-eyed terror.

Unable to articulate himself, he shouted again, "AWWW!" This time he pointed to his instrument panel. I leaned over to look at his fuel gauge. Empty. "Benze-e-e-e-ne!" he wailed. I just shook my head. "Ah, Majeed. We must keep a close eye on our fuel gauge."

Majeed dropped me on a dark street near Imam Khomeini Square, where the guidebook suggested I could find accommodations. He then sputtered off to find another driver with a fuel card.

Around two o'clock in the morning, I collapsed onto the bed of a cheap hotel room. An hour later I awoke dripping with sweat, my tongue clinging to the roof of my mouth. When I blinked, my eyes scraped against eyelids of emery cloth. Reaching for my water bottle, I remembered that I had lost it at the airport.

Is this room really hot, or do I have a wicked fever? I wondered. When I poked the chocolate bar on my nightstand, it oozed through the wrapper into a brown pool. The room had no windows and there was no thermostat to shut off the heater. I unplugged the refrigerator in the corner. Its compressor had been whirring and kicking off a lot of heat. That didn't entirely account for the high temperature, but it certainly didn't help. Crouching down, I opened the fridge door and lingered before the empty box for a few minutes. I wished that it were filled with bottles and bottles of cold water. I would drink them all. When the last of the cool air had escaped I stumbled through the heat, back to bed, where I passed a restless night dreaming of electric palm trees along the banks of a glacial river.

CHAPTER 35

Wintry air mopped my brow as I made my way through the wide streets of Tehran in search of a teahouse. The yellow leaves on the trees that lined the sidewalk rustled in the breeze. The buildings and most of the vehicles appeared modern, and the city seemed less chaotic than Damascus. Compared to Beirut, Tehran was more homogenous and less flashy.

That said, it had some interesting architecture. There was the Azadi Tower a forty-five-metre-high white marble monument that was built in 1971. It had a smooth archway through the middle and sweeping lines on either side that curved up to the sky. And there was the recently completed Milad Tower, which at 435 metres in height was the sixth-tallest tower in the world.

Zipping up my coat, I looked up at the pale sky and smiled. In the distance, through a bit of a haze, I could see the snow-covered Alborz Mountains. They were taller and more rugged than any I had seen on the trip so far.

City buses chirped their horns. They sounded like a bunch of cartoon robots whistling at a dog. Underpowered motorcycles with tall windshields zipped along, each one filtering through lines of cars at stoplights to get ahead when the light turned green. Instead of using gloves to keep warm, riders slipped their bare hands into thick mittens fastened to the bars to work the controls underneath. Most of them had open-faced helmets, allowing their moustaches to ripple in the wind. I wished the Oscillator could be here to see it all. But then, there were those mountains.

Whenever I pulled out my guidebook to check the map, people in long winter coats stepped up to help. One man even guided me on a ten-minute walk out of his way to the proper bus station before paying my fare and telling the driver where to let me off. I would find this sort of hospitality nearly every day in Iran.

Finally at the teahouse, I drew aside a curtain at the entrance to look in. Water bubbled out of a central fountain, pushing around rose petals floating in the pool below. Carpets, kilims, and pillows served as furniture. Most importantly, narghiles lined the stone walls on shelves or in little nooks. This is why I had come. But when I ordered a tea and a pipe, the waiter informed me that the pipes were merely for decoration. Religious leaders had recently banned the smoking of narghile in teahouses. At least I could have tea, he said.

Disappointed, I plopped onto a carpet near the fountain to write in my leather-bound journal. The waiter returned with several dishes filled with sweet, waxy dates, dehydrated bits of apple, and small white cookies. I hadn't ordered any of this, but I snacked on it anyway. Next he brought out a bowl of pomegranate seeds, a dish of steaming beets and another of white-and-yellow pudding that tasted like death. (For me, the scent of roses is linked to death because of my grandmother's funeral when I was four. Apparently that memory has also ruined the taste of rosewater, for that's what flavoured the pudding.)

In Tehran, women obeyed the national law that forces them to cover their heads, but most of them seemed to do it grudgingly. A small colourful scarf was enough to satisfy the morality police, and it was winter, anyway. The way they dressed would not have looked out of place on a cold day in any Canadian city. They were not shy about approaching me, either. As I sat with my journal and tea, a pair of ladies came over to join me. They giggled and even flirted with me a little in the teahouse. Before I left, they copied out part of a poem by the Persian poet Hafez into my notebook. I asked them what it said, but they claimed that it would lose its beauty if they translated it.

Later that afternoon I changed hotels to one that didn't try to suffocate me in the night. This one had a small office with a computer that I could use to check my e-mail. From time to time, an old man would walk in there, unroll his prayer mat, remove his shoes, and begin his prayers right in front of me. He would stand, bow, and prostrate himself as if he was the only person in the room, as if he was in the presence of God. At first I felt like I was intruding, but Muslims pray wherever they find space, and that's often in public.

Watching him, I began to re-examine my motivations for coming to Iran. Was it really some kind of spiritual search, or did I just want to see everything before some Western power reduced Iran to rubble?

If I had really come to find God, then I must be delusional. He wouldn't show himself to me, not even in this supposed theocracy. He wouldn't do that precisely because I'm not delusional, right?

It had always bothered me that God expects so much of us while refusing to show himself plainly. Some say that God can't reveal himself because that would nullify our faith, that precious commodity that God so desires. That never sat well with me, either. Why wouldn't love and obedience and faithfulness matter more? That would all be hard enough even if we knew God was there.

I posed that question once to a friend back in Canada after I was probably too drunk to discuss whatever else we were talking about – sports, maybe. We stood together in an alcove away from the dinner party crowd and she was trying to "encourage me" in my walk with God, or to make me stop bothering her with questions. She gave me the line about faith, and how that would disappear if God revealed himself.

"Yeah," I said, leaning against a wall to steady the room, "but what about love?"

"What about it?"

"Well, your parents. You love them, right?"

"Yeah."

"But you don't have to, see? And you obey them, and you work to maintain a relationship with them. And when you offend them you ask for forgiveness."

"Yeah. What's your point?"

"Well, have you ever doubted that they exist?"

I went on slurring about how even a quick skim of the Old Testament revealed countless stories of disobedience to God by people with apparently concrete evidence of his existence.

Still others claim that we do have this evidence today, that God actually has revealed himself though the act of creation. This universe is too complex to have just "happened," they say. These people often employ the Watchmaker Argument. The version I heard in high school has the added flourish of a walk in the woods and it goes like this: If you were in the forest and you found a wristwatch, you wouldn't go, "Wow, what an incredible natural formation!" Instead, you would know instinctively that this watch had a creator, because it was orderly and functional. It wouldn't even have to be as complex as that. It could be a simple thing like a cairn or in-ukshuk. You would see those stones and you would know that a man had arranged them that way. Now imagine the complexity of a human eye and explain how that could exist with no creator.

The same pastor who told me to get married also shared with me this overly simplistic argument. I listened to him but, as Richard Dawkins points out, this reasoning breaks down in the hands of an inquisitive five-year-old who keeps asking, "Why?"

"So," I said, playing the part of a bothersome toddler, "you're saying that the universe is obviously created because it has order?"

"Yes."

"But then, where did God come from?"

"Well, he's the crea-*tor*," he said, emphasizing the *tor* part.

"Yeah. I get that. But he has order. He is complex, right? So, you're admitting that order and complexity can exist without a creator."

"God is the creator."

And so one enters into the circular reasoning by which everything is explained but nothing makes sense. It's the same reasoning used to prove that the Bible is the word of God. How do I know? Because it says so in the Bible.

It's the same reasoning used to explain how the universe would only need ten thousand birthday candles on its cake. It looks older, you say? Well, do you think that God made Adam and Eve as infants in the Garden? Ha, ha. Of course he would have created them as sexually mature adults, in other words, with the appearance of age. What about the stars that we see, even though they are billions of light years away? Simple. The light was created billions of years into its journey.

Yes, and it's possible that the universe was born in 1979,

when Pink Floyd began recording "Comfortably Numb," and that all human history, literature, and memories from before that are artificial. Except that's not likely. And that's a reasonable response, I think, to say it's possible, but not likely.

What I couldn't admit to that pastor is that we do agree on lots of things, just not on how we get there. Believing that God exists and that he created everything is clearly ridiculous. But so is believing the scientific model espoused by Richard Dawkins et al. I guess what I'm saying is, when you consider the origins of life, when you consider eternity, when you consider infinity, no matter how you slice it you must believe at least one ridiculous thing. Let's all admit that.

While I was mulling this over I saw a bit of the city, a few museums and such, but mostly I trudged along wet streets watching trash float upon rivers of grey meltwater. Tehran was basically modern and clean, but the section where I lived was a bit run down.

In my memory, I've got this image of a rat paddling by on a raft of garbage. He was wearing a pirate hat, but that probably wasn't real. There were rats, though.

There was a brutal cold snap that year but, in spite of having to endure weather that actually killed people in Iran, motorcycle couriers still carried on. The tiny bikes bore up under incredible loads. One rider, bundled with hats and scarves so that only his eyes poked through, prepared to ride off with a load of fourteen full-sized truck tires on his bike. Another splashed along carrying a five-hundred-gallon drum, which I can only assume was empty. I'm sure that was real, but it was ridiculous, too.

Through a series of friendly encounters I received directions, cups of tea, city bus fare and help flagging down a taxi before arriving at the terminal, a circular building of concrete and glass that looked like a flying saucer in a field of buses. I climbed aboard a modern bus scheduled to depart for Esfahan, one of the cities I remembered Chikako had circled in her guidebook.

Plopping into the seat, I leaned my head against my backpack and closed my eyes.

"Excuse me," I heard a voice say. "Do you mind if I sit with you to practise my English?"

Smiling down at me stood a young man, well-dressed, with dark, wavy hair.

"My name is Farzad," he said. "May I?"

We chatted just long enough for me learn that Farzad was on break from university, before I set into motion events that nearly ruined his vacation.

"Do you think I have time to run to the toilet before we leave?" I asked.

Farzad frowned at his watch.

"I'll ask the driver," he said. "I better go along to make sure you find it quickly."

Before leaving the bus, Farzad told the driver that we would just pop into the station for a few minutes to use the WC. Was that all right? Yes, the driver assured him. There was still a line of passengers boarding the bus anyway. Fine. We will be back in no more than five minutes, Farzad said. OK? He held up five fingers to make himself very clear. Could he wait that long? Indeed.

Three and one-half minutes later (I timed it) Farzad and I trotted back to where the bus used to be, but it had gone. Second-guessing ourselves, we hurried along the circular row of buses that ringed the building, thinking that we had returned to the wrong platform. Every coach looked basically the same, although they had different religious slogans painted on the back. I couldn't remember what ours said.

Our pace quickened to a moderate jog through the parking lot. The sun beat down on us now, reflecting its heat off the tarmac.

"Can you hurry, please?" urged Farzad.

But I had made a pact with myself long ago that I would never run again unless fleeing some sort of natural disaster. Technically, this trotting business was against my beliefs. Besides, at twenty-five, Farzad was ten years my junior and he had no pack to hinder his stride. My pack bounced around in all directions, tugging at my shoulders and pulling my back farther out of alignment.

Anyway, our quest had incredible urgency, but no system. Farzad darted to and fro like a frightened gopher without a hole, searching the parking lot, running a few paces into the terminal, retreating out to the platform. In wide-eyed panic, he decided at last to approach the ticket desk.

There ensued a shouting match between Farzad and the ticket agents as I stood quietly dripping sweat onto the floor. Farzad tried to impress upon them how upset we both were, but I damaged his case as I wore an expression of relief now that we had stopped running. I tried to look angry. In fact I was angry, damn it.

I stood behind Farzad mimicking his gestures – pointing to the clock on the wall when he pointed, holding up five fingers when he did. When Farzad pointed to me, I nodded. Angrily. I tapped my watch and held up five fingers again. At this point Farzad noticed what I was doing and kindly asked me to go stand over there.

Eventually the ticket agents phoned the driver, who hadn't quite left the yard yet. He promised to wait for us at the gate.

"Can you hurry, please?" Farzad urged again, as we ran over hot pavement up a steep slope to catch our bus. When the driver opened the door, he smiled, and even chuckled as Farzad scolded him.

In the weeks that followed I learned that such asinine behaviour was characteristic of bus drivers. For example, on a blustery overnight journey I opted to stay on board while most passengers cleared off to stretch their legs at a roadside stop. The bus driver had a young assistant to collect fares, lift luggage and so on, and the driver asked him to check something at the front of the bus. The boy obeyed, although he was still groggy from having just woken up. He stepped outside, walked to the front, and stooped out of view with his head very near the front bumper, where the horn was located. The driver honked the horn.

The boy jumped like he had been shot in the ass with a pellet gun. The driver jumped, too. Then they yelled at each other through the windshield.

The driver soon forgot about his helper as he continued messing with controls, testing this and that. The boy walked back. As the boy lifted his foot to step inside, at that very moment, the driver shut the door.

The boy had to knock to enter, but he didn't do that right away. It seemed like he waited about long enough to do a slow ten count with, I imagine, his hand pressed up against his face. Knock, knock, knock

Arriving in Esfahan, Farzad insisted on going with me to find a hotel, but he turned his nose up at my selection. "It's too dirty," he said.

"It's how I roll," I replied. "It's cheap."

However, the manager would not allow me to check in either, citing a special situation. "You must first register with the police," he said. He refused to elaborate.

Farzad and I walked to a tourist police office, where we learned that the authorities had restricted foreigner access to a mere seven approved hotels. I looked at the list. "I can't afford to stay at any of these places," I said. "You must," said the captain. "There's a special situation in Esfahan right now."

Though the captain would not elaborate either, Farzad collected more information from another officer. The story ran like this:

A known criminal, Kazem Shafiyee, had escaped from prison. He managed this with the help of his mother, who had smuggled a gun to him in a sandwich.

"She put the gun in a sandwich?" I interrupted. Farzad nodded.

Using the gun, Shafiyee broke out and vanished. Subsequently, the police arrested members of his family for aiding and abetting him, at which point the criminal threatened to start killing people unless authorities released his family. To prove his point, he murdered a police officer. Next – and this is the part that affected foreigners – he shot a French tourist a few days earlier in the very bus station in which Farzad and I had just arrived. Shafiyee warned police that he would do it again.

I heard versions of the same story throughout my time in Iran, though I found no reputable source to verify the wacky details. The escape with the gun sandwich sounded like bad fiction, but the rest of it was true. While travelling with his fiancée, a French tourist named Julien Van Waesberghe lost his life in an Esfahan bus terminal for no good reason.

CHAPTER 36

When I woke up, it occurred to me that staying in an expensive hotel had perks. The price included breakfast, for example. Besides, "expensive" is a relative term. Even though the room exceeded my accommodation budget, it was still cheaper than a Winnipeg haircut.

Breakfast came right to my door on a silver tray. Nice fried eggs, soft flatbread, and a pot of steaming tea. Picking up a lump of hard sugar from the bowl, I dipped it into my cup before popping it into my mouth. There it stayed, on my tongue, as it dissolved a bit more with every sip of tea.

The room had a firm bed and its own sink. It was clean. A prayer mat stood rolled up in the corner, and on the table sat a basket of clay tablets. These must be the tablets that Lesley Hazleton mentions in *After the Prophet*, where she writes, "The Shia faithful still gather dust from the sandy soil of Najaf, the city surrounding Ali's gold-domed shrine a hundred miles south of Baghdad, then press it into small clay tablets that they place in front of them as they pray so that wherever in the world a Shia prostrates himself in prayer, the soil his forehead touches is sacred soil." A mark on the wall indicated the direction of Mecca.

With no English programming on television, I gathered as much information as a cat pawing at the screen, but I watched anyway. Actually, I did find a program that ran an

English news ticker, where I learned that the "U.S. sponsors terror cells in Iraq," and that "Soon the Zionist Regime of Israel will be cut like a tumour from the Middle East." The ticker also said that the Esfahan bus stop killer had been apprehended, but I didn't place much faith in the information.

Switching off the television, I walked to the lavatory located across from the reception desk. I nodded to the clerk before stepping inside.

Like most Middle Eastern toilets, this one comprised a hole in the floor with two footpads on either side. To use it, you stood on the pads and squatted down, resting on your haunches. To the westerner, this seems awkward at first; so awkward, in fact, that some hotels offer a "Western Toilet," a more conventional fixture of the type you would find in North America. Even these, however, often had no seat – just the bowl.

As for me, I had no issue with the typical Middle Eastern privy. In fact, once I got used to it, I found squatting like that quite comfortable. Relaxing, even. It offers a more natural position to conduct your business, and I often chose it over the "Western Toilet" anyway.

One thing I never cared for, though, was that you could not flush your toilet paper, because of the narrow plumbing. It would plug the system. Instead, you placed it into a plastic basket for someone to come in and empty later.

What I liked even less were the bathrooms like this one that had no baskets. No toilet paper. Just a hose.

In time, I would come to appreciate this system, too, but for the moment I found myself on the bottom of a steep learning curve. When I had finished, I remained squatting while I reached for the coil of hose on the floor. Beads of water collected on its surface from a previous user. It had a waxy coating of some kind that transferred to my hands when I handled it. At least this one had a nozzle with a trigger to start the flow. A nice touch, I thought. Some of them free flow like a garden hose. With one hand, I bunched up my pants to keep them dry, while aiming the hose with the other.

Having shot water pistols at targets in a summer fair, I knew that direct hits are rare. A clean hit would be especially difficult in this case because the target was behind me. Positioning the nozzle by feel and intuition, I paused for a moment before pulling the trigger. It required commitment. Then, at the last second, I bowed my head, craning my neck between my legs in an effort to see where the hose pointed.

That's how a ricochet of water hit me square in the face. Even then, the stream carried enough force to hit the door and splatter throughout the room, raining down on me in a fine mist. Apparently, the hose could also be used in an emergency to scatter an angry crowd.

I shouted as the water blasted off the door. How would that have sounded to the hotel clerk? Never mind. Still squatting, I spit a bunch of times before wiping the water from my face.

Fortunately, the stream only ricocheted off my pants and so carried with it little or no sediment. The downside is that I now had a pair of soaking wet pants around my ankles. After cleaning up as best I could, I waddled past the clerk to my room.

CHAPTER 37

Like nutrients in soil that receives too much rain, nearly all the colour had leached from the sky, leaving it pale blue overhead and the colour of cotton at the horizon. The white sun reflected off concrete sidewalks and beige buildings, causing me to squint. In an effort to stand out a little less, I had picked up the habit of leaving my sunglasses behind. In fact, I had left them in Syria.

It was a wintry day here, but it felt like a pleasant autumn afternoon back home. I could stay outside comfortably in a sweater. Some men wore clothes of a similar style to mine, while many others wore suit jackets with collared shirts. The older men wore dress pants and the younger ones wore jeans.

And then there were the counter-culture set, the teenagers dressed as American rock stars from 1987. They wore tight pants, spiky hair, and gaudy sunglasses. I just wanted to shake them by the shoulders and go, "Get a grip, man! We tried all that."

As for the women, some of them wore chadors, but very few covered their faces. Young women often wore blue jeans beneath long coats, the hems of which typically hung just above the knee. Just like in Tehran, some of their outfits would have blended into the scene in any North American city.

On my way to Imam Square, four young girls, in high

school probably, giggled their way over to speak to me. The bravest one had a Band-Aid across the bridge of her nose, and she spoke English quite well. We chatted for a few moments while the others stood by, whispering to one another and smiling at me with bright eyes. Occasionally, one of them would throw out an English sentence she had learned in class. I felt rather uncomfortable, like I might be breaking some sort of law by speaking with them, but the girls were bold.

Again, when I arrived at the square, three young women approached me. These ladies were older, of college age, slender and beautiful with delicate hands. They were students of architecture, they said, and they were taking photos in the square for a class. They offered to show me around, but when the teacher noticed the girls speaking with me he called them away sharply, leaving me to wander alone.

An impressive expanse of land lay within the rectangular perimeter of a two-storey arcade. You could mark out ten American football fields within that space if you placed them side by side, and you'd still have room for end-zone bleachers.

Large pools of grey water featured rows of fountains, arcing streams towards their centres with as much imagination as a common lawn sprinkler. A child ran along the edge of the water, teetering for a moment with outstretched arms before his mother snatched him back.

I looked up past the water. The colossal dome and high minarets of the Imam Mosque dominated the architecture on the southern end of the square, appearing through the haze as a blue silhouette against a white sky. Beyond the archway in the southern wall, the actual mosque angled off to the side to line up with Mecca.

From there, I ambled south towards the river to see Esfahan's famous bridges. It's these pedestrian bridges, along with a vast bazaar and the striking architecture of the Imam Square and surrounding mosques, that inspired the sixteenth-century rhyme, "Esfahan is half the world." Well, the translation doesn't rhyme, nor does it quite make sense, but it does sound grand.

Along the way, a young man in a suit jacket edged up beside me. He said he was a doctor and then, basically out of nowhere he said, "I used to go to Russia for sex."

"Russia for sex?" I said.

He nodded. "That was before the ban," he said. Then he catalogued for me what he could and could not do with girlfriends in Iran. "Here, maybe kiss and maybe boobs. You know boobs?" he asked. I nodded. "Maybe, if she agrees, sex OK. But then big problem with police."

He looked at me, raising his eyebrows slightly. "And you?" he said, "What about Canada? Can you have sex with girls?"

"Well, she has to agree to have sex in Canada, too," I said. "But, if she does, then yeah. There's no problem with police."

The doctor smiled, taking a deep breath through his nose. "I want to go to Canada," he said.

CHAPTER 38

Farzad showed me around Esfahan later that night. We walked back to the river, criss-crossing the same pedestrian bridges now illuminated against the dark. At the Khaju Bridge, men gathered in the soft light beneath one of the arched tunnels to sing, their voices echoing from stone and mortar.

Lower down, two stone lions stood facing each other from opposite banks. Farzad guided me down to one of the lions and positioned me behind it.

"Look at the lion on the other shore," said Farzad. "Can you see the eyes?"

The beast was black with shadow, but it stared back at me with fiery eyes.

"Yeah, they're glowing," I said. I figured that they must have put lights in the lion's head. "That's cool."

"But there are no lights," Farzad said with a sly grin. "No one knows why the eyes glow."

I walked around to inspect the face of the lion in front of me. No lights. When we walked across the bridge, however, the eyes of that lion glowed, too.

"No one knows," Farzad smiled.

"Well, obviously it's just a reflection from one of these other lights," I said, looking around.

"Yes, but which one?" he asked. "And how can one light create two eyes?"

Farzad had a point. None of the lights stood in the correct spot to create such perfect reflection off the face of either statue.

"Hmm. Interesting."

We strolled back along the river as Farzad picked up a conversation he had initiated on the bus the day before.

"It would be better for us if America came and took over," he said. He spoke openly about politics, which surprised me. In Syria, people guarded their words much more carefully.

"We want America to change our government," he said again.

"Yeah," I said, "you should ask someone from Iraq how that's going over there."

We walked in silence for a moment.

"It's never clean," I said. "There was a time when an invading nation just carpet bombed everything, killing everyone. You'd be dead. Your family would be dead. But the regime would change.

"In these times, you have to distinguish between a government and the people. The world wants to see enemy leadership and their military removed with small numbers of civilian casualties. Of course that's ideal, but it makes war inefficient. It prolongs it. And then, when the invading nation pulls out, there's the civil war to follow."

It's more complex than all that, but I had trouble envisioning anything except two scenarios – total destruction, or a long, ugly campaign. Besides, the U.S. and England had already toppled an Iranian leader once before, not so long ago. Indirectly, they were responsible for the current administration that Farzad hated.

In the early 1950s, democratically elected leader Mohammad Mossadegh sought to nationalize Iran's oil reserves, leaving more money for Iranians at the expense of

British oil companies. That seemed like a good move to everyone in Iran, but the English took exception to the idea.

Under the Eisenhower administration, the U.S. cooperated with England to undermine support for Mossadegh. The CIA operated out of the American embassy in Tehran, and ousted Mossadegh using what amounted to a highly effective smear campaign. He spent the remainder of his life under house arrest.

His successor, Shah Mohammed Reza, denationalized oil reserves, allowing American and British investors back in the game. Years later, he also ran the Iranian economy into the dust. That, and his policies of reform in a conservative nation, led to street riots, which the Shah crushed with brutal force.

The protests continued, however. Eventually the reins of power slipped from his grasp into the hands of another leader, a leader who promised a nation free from foreign influence. A nation that would take its direction from God. That was the Islamic Revolution of 1979, and its leader was Ayatollah Khomeini – a man who, until his death, remained a thorn in the side of the U.S., dubbing America "the Great Satan."

CHAPTER 39

Colour returned to the sky in the morning, and the blue tiles of the Imam Mosque rose up to meet it. The sky blended so well with the mosque that the heavens could have passed for a vast dome above the courtyard. The pointed archway was rimmed with decorative trim of looping columns, like swirls of soft turquoise ice cream. Above that, a crisp rectangle of royal blue framed the doorway. There were subtle differences between the two pillars on either side of the door. This was done intentionally, I was told, to rob the building of perfect symmetry. The reason: to show that only God could make something perfect. That may have been a lesson in humility, but to me it smacked of arrogance.

Once inside, I stood with my back to the main sanctuary and faced the entrance and turquoise minarets. The ablution pool, a pool of still water used for ritual cleansing, reflected white calligraphy and yellow floral patterns from the walls of the main courtyard.

Behind me, another yawning archway sandwiched between two more minarets stood before the blue dome of the main sanctuary. Sanctuary. Now I had "She Sells Sanctuary" by the Cult stuck in my head. What the heck? I had the place almost to myself, so I pulled out my air guitar (good thing I brought it along). After plugging into an invisible amp, I did a quick sound check and adjusted the levels. I didn't jump around and play that much, though. Mostly I just held the pose from the cover of their *Sonic Temple* album.

My guidebook said that you could hear a series of distinct echoes if you stamped on the black paving stones in the exact centre of the main sanctuary. It claimed that scientists have recorded dozens of them, but that only about the first seven or so are audible to the human ear.

Positioning myself on the stones, I looked up at the ceiling. It towered above me to a height of over thirty-six metres. I stamped my foot.

"She Sells Sanctuary" got bumped by the theme to *Chariots of Fire* – that's what the echoes reminded me of, that reverberating percussion. I stamped again. *Chariots of Fire.* Or, wait. What else did it remind me of? Stamp. It sounded like Steve Austin, the Six Million Dollar Man, just ran by really, really fast.

A young Iranian man stood in the corner watching me stamp on the floor. He smiled and came over to say hello.

"We don't see many tourists from the West anymore," he said. I told him about my problems getting a visa for Iran.

"Excuse me," he said, still smiling, "but it is not easy for us if we want to visit Canada, either."

When I had finished looking around, I left the mosque. Outside, men readied the courtyard for Friday prayers. They rolled out layers of tarpaulin, padding, and, finally, soft red carpet. Watching them, I thought back to the last church service I had attended. It was earlier in the trip, in Croatia. I went with a friend who I hadn't seen in over a decade.

Twelve years earlier I had volunteered a token effort in the region, rebuilding some damaged buildings in Croatia and Bosnia. The Bosnian War had just ended, but there was still enough horror clinging to the rubble to create a palpable sense of evil. Another religious war. That was the first time I had wrestled with God – or rather, with absolutes. When you're young, sometimes that line gets blurry.

Heavy rain turned to drizzle as I approached Rijeka. The road felt greasy beneath my wheels, and my front tire nearly slipped out from beneath me on a few turns. They used a limestone mix on their roads in the former Yugoslavia, and that makes everything dangerously slippery when wet.

I rode slowly, hoping that landmarks memorized a decade ago would lead me to the train station where I was to meet my old friend. I knew Teo from the Life Centre, the place where I had volunteered in 1995.

Teo was there to greet me. He had the same infectious smile that I remembered from years ago, a smile so broad that his cheeks pushed his eyes shut. He hadn't changed, except that now his cheeks had some extra bulk to better close his eyes with when he smiled. After securing the bike, we climbed into his car.

Teo used to pastor a church on the southern tip of Croatia's western peninsula, and on that morning he had agreed to help out with music. On the drive, we caught up on each other's lives. We also talked about the mood of the region since the war.

"The people are not forgetting, they are not forgiving," said Teo. "But they are not furious, either."

We drove in silence through a long tunnel, emerging in Croatia's wine region. Vineyards, olive groves, and orchards slipped past on the other side of the glass. At cutbanks in the road, white stones poked out of red soil. In this rain, rivulets of muddy water streaked them like blood on exposed bone.

"The earth is red and the stones are white," said Teo, "but people just call it 'red rock' anyway."

The church could seat around forty, but there were only

eight people there, ten including Teo and me. I sat in the back, looking over the congregation. There was a young family, an elderly widow, and a couple. The couple sat with an empty chair between them. The woman never smiled and the man texted on his cell phone for the entire service.

The proceedings unfolded in Croatian with formulaic precision, opening with an upbeat song (clapping and swaying permitted, but keep your hands down) followed by a downtempo piece (bowed heads and closed eyes, here you may raise one hand if you like, but we'd prefer if you didn't). Then, to prepare hearts for the message, the final chorus was sung repeatedly, getting slower and slower with each lap until every syllable dragged on for a second, a cappella.

Once everyone had grown sufficiently sombre, the pastor stood to deliver the message. Beneath his suit jacket, he wore a dress shirt streaked with all the hues of a pastel rainbow. This is what Joseph's coat of many colours would have looked like if Jacob bought it from Zellers in 1983.

He seemed to be a competent orator, but he only got three people to smile at his jokes – the two children and their mother.

The Croatian church was Baptist, like the kind I used to attend in Alberta. I say used to, because although some of my friends still went there, I had no intention of going back. I had been getting more and more detached from the messages that the pastor delivered – one Sunday in particular stands out in my memory. Following a sermon that poked at a theme of sexual purity (read: sexual abstinence out of wedlock), another man in the congregation raised his hand. He was a married man, and although no one knew this at the time, the marriage would soon fall apart. For whatever reason, he chose to single me out for an example.

"That's fine for you to keep your sexual impulses in check," he said to the pastor, who was also married, "but what about young single guys like Jeremy?"

Everyone turned to look at me in the back row. I smiled and waved. It was a small group of forty people or so, and I knew them all fairly well. Now, I wasn't exactly out there whoring it up on the weekends, but people knew that I had girlfriends occasionally, and I guess they made certain assumptions.

That's not the point. In a context where people considered a longing look at a woman to be adultery, I had definitely committed adultery several times already that morning.

"Well," the pastor replied, "you need to turn your sexual frustration into prayerful meditation."

Those were his exact words.

Suddenly I realized that this man either didn't understand sexual frustration, or he knew less about prayerful meditation than he thought. In high school, I spent hours on my knees wetting my pillow with tears and screaming into it for God to forgive my lust. After a while, pleading for forgiveness every single day seemed hollow. Was I really sorry for staring after girls if I kept doing it? Sometimes, in my daydreams, I imagined kissing them. How awful. Sometimes, in my dreams, they were naked.

Late at night in the privacy of my room, those thoughts occasionally manifested themselves into acts that I assumed were abhorrent to God (and which definitely caused my mother to do lots of laundry). As I was trapped in Christian high-school land, I assumed that I was the only impure soul among my peers. This was a secret unholy shame that I, and I alone, must bear.

So I took the next step in prayer. I asked God to kill my sexual urges, which I felt powerless to control. And if God would not kill my desire, then I prayed that he would, in his mercy, kill me.

Night after night I prayed for death. I cried and asked to die, basically because I liked girls. I prayed that the Lord would call me home because if I remained on his earth, in this body, with these desires, I would bring him shame nearly every waking moment of every day.

When mornings came, the fight continued. If I caught myself thinking about sex I quickly substituted one desire for another. When sexual imagery appeared in my mind, I would replace it with graphic images of my own death. That's fucked up.

I would imagine disembowelments with samurai swords, crushing blows from falling boulders, drowning. Rather than dwelling on what it might feel like to receive a warm kiss on my neck, or a tender stroke on my skin from a caring partner, I imagined the cool steel of a shotgun barrel and the oily taste of metal as it pressed against the roof of my mouth. Then I imagined the final blast that would ultimately and forever clear my mind of sexual imagery. This seemed to be the lesser of two evils.

It seemed biblical, too. After all, there's that part where Jesus goes: "But I tell you that anyone who looks at a woman lustfully has already committed adultery with her in his heart. If your right eye causes you to sin, gouge it out and throw it away. It is better for you to lose one part of your body than for your whole body to be thrown into hell. And if your right hand causes you to sin, cut it off and throw it away. It is better for you to lose one part of your body than for your whole body to go into hell."

Of course, no person in his or her right mind would lop off a body part because of that passage (that would be taking the Bible too literally) but, historically speaking, it's not without precedent. Most people water that passage down a bit by saying, "Jesus just meant that if you are sinning, then you should take drastic actions to counter that." Or the whole point is that no matter how careful or good you are, you have sinned and therefore need forgiveness. Like, you think you're being good by not committing adultery? Well, you're still not good enough.

Fine. But that's not how my high-school mind worked it out. On the other hand, I wasn't about to cut anything off, either. Eventually I did take a knife to my body, carving the words "No More" so deeply into my shoulder that the scar remains to this day. (Now when people ask what it means, I tell them, "No more cutting myself with a utility knife.")

Anyway, that passage justified my suicidal fantasies. I pointed an imaginary gun at what I considered to be the problem – my brain – and I pulled the trigger.

Certain biblical characters may have contemplated suicide as well, I reasoned. At least, there are a few who wanted to die. Like the Prophet Elijah, for example, who asked God to take his life. Or the Prophet Jonah, who claimed that he was angry enough to die. And of course, who could forget Paul, who famously wrote, "For to me to live is Christ, and to die is gain."

After all, each human life is just one spark in a giant ignition coil. When compared with eternity, the brevity of this existence is absurd. It's a practice life in which you have seconds to figure out the next billion years, which are only the beginning. If you believe that you'll live forever, then this life just doesn't matter. It all boils down to time, and specifically, eternity.

In his novel *Even Cowgirls Get the Blues*, Tom Robbins put it this way: "We dilute and hobble our most genuinely felt impulses with the idea, whether fervently held or naggingly suspected, that after death there is something else, and that that something may be endless, and that the correctness of our behavior in 'this' life may determine how we fare in the 'next' one ... Thus, whether it is in danger of stopping and catching us with our pants down, or whether it runs on forever and demands that we busy ourselves preparing for the next station on the long ride, either way, time prevents us from living authentically."

It certainly has had that effect on me.

CHAPTER 40

Back at the bus terminal, I bought a ticket for Yazd. I was early. Now that I had the ticket, I'd have to wait over an hour before departure.

Never mind. I could easily spend that much time wandering around in the sun. Maybe I'd find a nice park in which to sit and write. As I headed for the door, a large man in a brown suit intercepted me. With an outstretched hand, he invited me to the waiting room.

"Please," he said.

"Thank you," I replied. "But I'd prefer to walk around."

"No."

"Why not?"

"Dangerous."

"Why is it dangerous?"

He wouldn't say. He just motioned again to the waiting room and said, "Please."

We stood facing each other in the foyer, the man still blocking my exit as I considered the options. Who was this guy? Here he was, forbidding me to leave, yet he hadn't identified himself as someone with any authority.

I wondered if he would physically stop me if I tried to go. I took a small step towards the door. The man edged over into my path. I paused, searching his face for clues as to what he might do next. He was stone-faced. I took a larger step to go around him, then another to force his hand. He turned with me, but yielded to let me pass.

In the parking lot, I stopped to look back at the station. The man in the brown suit had followed me to the door. He stood there, glowering. Several men stood near him, two of them in police uniform. They all watched me.

Now I didn't know what to do. Was I about to stumble into a legitimately dangerous area? Maybe I should not leave the station after all.

This probably still had to do with the bus stop killer. The news ticker on TV claimed he had been apprehended, but that could have been a lie. In all likelihood I would be all right in this neighbourhood as long as I stayed alert. What were the odds that the killer would single me out, anyway? Pretty low. Had he been watching the bus station? Probably not.

Leaving the parking lot, I walked stiffly along a plain street with grocery stores and shops. My eyes darted about, looking for anything out of the ordinary. Admittedly, Mr. Brown Suit had made me nervous. As I turned to watch a blackened mechanic sling curses against a Peugeot, something caught my attention out of the corner of my eye. A flash of movement. Someone was following me.

A tingle ran down my spine. Fighting the instinct to wheel around, I forced myself to move slowly. If I was being followed, I did not want to tip off my stalker that I was onto him. Waiting a beat, I glanced back down the sidewalk. A young man in blue jeans and a dark sweater was running straight at me. His gait betrayed a sense of urgency, but he wore a blank expression. I couldn't tell if he had targeted me or if he was just hurrying along somewhere. He did slow to a walk when I looked at him, though. That was weird.

I turned to leave, straining to hear footsteps approaching

at my back. All was quiet. After a few paces, I stopped to look in another shop window, casting another glance over my shoulder to gauge if the man had closed the gap between us. He had. In fact he now followed close behind, just on the edge of realistic handgun range, I thought. When I stopped, he stopped to look in a window, too.

I moved on, walking slowly – so slowly that the man would look rather conspicuous behind me unless he passed. I wanted to flush him out or force a conflict. All this buildup was too stressful. It worked. The man stepped closer.

My muscles tightened. I clenched my fists and got ready to drop my pack for a scuffle. But when the man caught up to me after all my loitering, he just passed right on by.

I stood still on the sidewalk to create some separation between me and the man. I could feel my heart beating. He was ahead of me now, which meant that I could breathe easy. Only, when I resumed walking, he slowed his pace just as I had done.

That's when I relaxed completely. To be on the safe side, I had entertained the possibility that this man was a threat, but all along I had suspected that he was a policeman sent to protect me. Now I knew. Soon we found ourselves walking side by side in awkward silence. The man continued the charade that he was merely going in the same direction. Wasn't it strange that we kept bumping into each other like this?

Except that running up to a stranger, following him, and then walking with him in complete silence is anti-social behaviour. Attempting to salvage the wreckage, the man tried to strike up a conversation.

"*Salam,*" he said.

"*Salam.*"

"From where?"

"Canada."

He nodded. That exhausted our ability to communicate. I knew one or two other words. For example, in Iran, many people said, "thank you" in French.

I stopped to shake the man's hand and said, "*Merci.*" I said it in such a way that also meant, "Goodbye."

The man understood. He smiled, shook my hand, and then turned back towards the bus station.

Ducking down a side street, I found a park with pine trees and thick green grass. There was one deciduous tree with smooth bark that had shed most of its leaves for winter, but the shrubs, which had been formed into basket shapes around wire frames, still had most of their green foliage. As I wrote in my journal, I kept a nervous eye on my surroundings, but with all that shifty-eyed observation the only thing that looked suspicious in the park was me. After a few minutes, I concentrated more on my journal.

No one followed me on the walk back, and it was still early when I arrived at the terminal. The station had a yard out back with a path and some trees. I went outside to look around.

As I left the building, two men followed me. One of them was the young man with the dark sweater from the street. I liked him. He was comically inept at being sneaky. Whenever we made eye contact, he nodded. Once I even got him to wave.

His partner was more professional. He wore black pants and a white turtleneck. Together, they shadowed me all over that tiny yard. They were trying to be discreet, but it was impossible in such a small space – especially because I was messing with them.

I moved erratically. The faster I walked, the closer they followed for fear of losing me. Once I even got Dark Sweater to follow me around a tree for two revolutions.

Next I paced back and forth in shorter and shorter lines until I had us all confined to within an area about the size of an average hot tub. There we were. Three grown men standing very close in an empty yard, all of us pretending that we didn't notice each other.

Then I had a sobering thought. Why it occurred to me so late, I don't know, for it was fairly obvious. These men were not there for my amusement. They were being paid to do something rather more important than that. They were there for my protection. Suddenly ashamed of my behaviour, I returned inside to wait like a normal person.

I should have taken the situation more seriously right from the start. After all, a man had been killed in that station just over a week ago. Although I didn't learn this until months later, that man had also been waiting for a bus to Yazd.

CHAPTER 41

My eyes lit up when the manager of the Silk Road Hotel in Yazd offered me a complimentary "Iranian Beer."

"Yes, please," I said. The rules regarding alcohol must be lax in some tourist spots, I figured. A beer would be lovely.

I tipped a dose into my mouth as the manager looked on. He appeared anxious to have my opinion of his Iranian Beer. Had he looked away, even for a moment, I might have returned it to the bottle. Rather, with pursed lips and bulging cheeks, I nodded. Eventually I had to swallow.

"Interesting," I said. Although the beverage had some beer-like characteristics – smell, appearance – it tasted like sparkling apple juice long past its expiration date. Also, and more importantly, it contained no alcohol.

Sorely disappointed, I took the bottle to my room to release the contents into the sink. I flushed it down the drain with tap water. Yazd was a dry town in more than one sense. Out here in the desert, even the water smelled of dust, like the first drops of rain on a gravel road.

Breakfast lasted for hours the next morning and every day thereafter. It was a social event, and it was at that table where I learned about the Silk Road's ominous reputation.

"It's the Black Hole," said one traveller. Others nodded.

"If you check in, you can kiss the rest of Iran goodbye, because you're staying right here for the rest of your life."

"Like Hotel California," I said.

"Exactly."

It was true. During my stay, I rolled off the couches a few times to walk through the old city, or to see a mosque, but the majority of my time was spent right there in that courtyard. The owners had designed the hostel to attract western travellers, keeping us, and our money, from leaving the building.

A traditional house converted to a hostel, it had Iranian flavour, yet it felt safe and familiar, too. Christmas decorations hung from the walls. They even had a real Christmas tree. That's a rare sight in the Middle East.

At any given time, half a dozen travellers could be found lounging by the central fountain on wooden platforms like queen-sized beds. Together, we spent our time on those beds sharing travel stories, drinking tea, and reading.

Each daybed had a thin kilim to protect the surface, and several round pillows to facilitate long hours of inactivity. Those pillows had an insidious way of absorbing time, for breakfast became morning tea, which transitioned into lunch. Afternoon tea followed, and then dinner, before we realized it was too late to see the town. At night, before bed, we huddled like kittens around a cylindrical gas burner that reminded me of the robot from *Lost in Space*.

The ease with which one could lose a day in that manner had something to do with comfortable surroundings and good company, but mostly I blame the menu. It contained Iranian dishes that the budget traveller could afford, like camel stew or *fesenjan* – meatballs drenched in a dark pomegranate and walnut sauce. We never left the beds to order, and we never reached for our wallets. Meals were charged to our rooms, making it all too easy to stay.

Fortunately, sometimes a traveller would burn his tongue while sipping tea and snap out of his torpor. If he acted fast, that person might drag one or two others into the outside world.

On one such occasion, two French travellers rescued me. I found myself bewildered and squinting at the sky in the dirt parking lot outside the hotel. Grey clouds carried with them just enough rain to tease the desert. Water would not touch the ground that day. Soon, we were all ascending a dusty slope towards the Tower of Silence.

"Are you sure you wouldn't rather go back to the hotel?" someone suggested.

"No. This is more important."

The mound of brown earth that we climbed rose from the desert plain, topping out into a flat summit. Our taxi driver followed us enthusiastically at first, but he abandoned the climb for a cigarette about a quarter of the way up. From the top, we could see him picking his way back to the car, which appeared as a black speck on a sweeping blanket of beige.

The tower, built from brick and mortar the same colour as the land, emerged from the hill like a natural formation. It was short and round with an open ceiling. A small portal, crumbling from neglect, led inside.

As the others scrambled through the entryway, I walked the perimeter of the building. The Tower of Silence. I liked that. It stood alone up here in the wind, overlooking barren plains and distant mountains. In the other direction, marks of industry could be seen, but even if the encroachment continued it would never reach the tower. At present, there were no tourist kiosks, no gondolas or easy paths to access it, and I imagine there never will be.

Climbing through the wall, I caught up with Alexandre

and Benoît. They embodied a romanticized stereotype of the vagabond adventurer. They were both costumed in Hollywood war reporter attire. Whenever I took their picture, the camera saw them as a pair of GQ models with wind-tousled hair. Most images featured them gazing to the horizon as if stoically bearing up under the burden of physical perfection. Fortunately, I found no evidence that they believed their own press. They were down-to-earth and good-humoured.

"The Tower of Silence," said Ben, "it's Zoroastrian." He pointed to a round pit in the middle of the floor. "This is where they brought the dead."

Rather than defiling the earth by burying the deceased, Zoroastrians sat the dead at the edge of the pit to have their flesh picked away by vultures. Priests monitored the ghastly spectacle to determine which eye the birds removed first. If they plucked out the right eye, it meant a better eternal rest for the departed soul.

This tower and others like it remained in use until as recently as the 1960s, a fact that made me think of long-haired corpses in Grateful Dead T-shirts. What makes the fact surprising is that people have practiced Zoroastrianism in the region since at least 550 BCE. Around that time, the belief system grew in status to become the state religion of Persia. Although estimates place the current number of active followers at a paltry two hundred thousand, Zoroastrianism's influence can still be felt around the world for one important reason – Zoroastrians invented monotheism.

That is to say, Zoroaster, the religion's founder, gets credit for the idea. All the guidebooks say this. However, whether he invented the concept of one all-powerful god, or whether he discovered that truth, depends on your point of view. I know many people who claim that monotheism was invented by God. Either way, Zoroaster's teachings seem to have influenced subsequent monotheistic religions that sprang up in the region, including Judaism, Islam, and Christianity.

The Zoroastrians influenced the Abrahamic religions in spite of a traditional estimate that Zoroaster was born more than one thousand years after Abraham. The guidebooks say this, too, without further explanation.

They could elaborate by saying that there is no consensus for Zoroaster's date of birth. Even excluding the most extreme estimates (as nearly everyone does), which put it at 6000 BCE, some scholars believe that he at least predated Abraham, if only just. This is often supported by the ancient language he used in writing portions of the Avesta – the oldest and most holy book for the Zoroastrians.

Another explanation for how the Zoroastrians get credit for monotheism is that the Abrahamic religions didn't start out that way. Not exactly. Abraham, and generations that followed, allowed for the possibility that other gods existed. They just understood their god to be the boss.

The God of Abraham at least held sway over Zoroastrian scholars and priests at the one definitive moment when their stories overlap, according to early Christian texts. In spite of praying to a different deity, several men of Zoroastrian order foretold the birth of Jesus, the Bible claims. They travelled from afar to worship the newborn with gifts of gold, frankincense, and myrrh. The Zoroastrians called their priests Magi. Christians commonly refer to them as the Three Wise Men.

CHAPTER 42

The day trip to the Tower of Silence broke the inertia. I still lazed around a lot in Yazd, but every day from then on I made an effort to get out and see something of the town.

Stepping outside, I faced the blue archway of the Jameh Mosque, with its two lofty minarets. Here in the old city, the mosque had the market cornered on vivid colour in an otherwise brown maze of smooth walls built from sun-dried bricks and plaster.

These walls closed in on each other to form alleys that meandered like gentle streams. They flaunted feminine curves as if to compensate for the real women of Yazd, who hid their figures behind the chador.

Few cities in Iran were more conservative than Yazd. Many women wore the niqab to cover their faces. In the old city, doorways to private homes featured two knockers – on the left, a heavy phallic one that dropped with a thud for men to use, and a round one on the right, for women, that clicked lightly. If a man knocked on the door, then a man should answer, or at least the women inside should cover up appropriately.

It was a small detail, but a tangible product of male sexual insecurity, according to Switters, a character from a Tom Robbins novel. In *Fierce Invalids Home from Hot Climates*, Switters muses that these insecurities "... among men of the Middle East achieved titanic, even earth-changing proportions; insecurities that had spawned veils, shaven heads, clitoridectomies, house arrest, segregation, macho posturing, and three major religions. *The women hereabouts must have really been something!* thought Switters."

It may take weeks for a traveller to build up the resolve to leave the Silk Road Hotel. Predictably, my first attempt failed. When I arrived at the bus station with my backpack, I learned that the coach to Shiraz was full. I could have waited for the next one or found a bus for another destination, but when I heard the news I could hardly suppress a grin. I could now return to the Silk Road without shame, satisfied that at least I had tried to leave.

"Ha!" someone shouted when I returned. "Couldn't do it, hey?"

"We knew you'd be back!" said another.

I just smiled. I took the same room as I had before. After another meal of camel stew, I took a city bus out to visit a Zoroastrian fire temple. There's a fire there, now behind a glass wall, that is said to have been burning continuously since the fifth century CE. Zoroastrian priests have attended to the fire all this time, and they keep stoking it with wood to this day.

After looking around, I rushed right back to the hotel. It would be my last night there, and I wanted to enjoy it.

A cold wind snapped at the fabric roof that stretched across the courtyard. I sat by the gas heater long into the night, reading a tattered copy of *A Farewell to Arms* and trying to work up the resolve to leave the next day. I listened to the low roar of flame, feeling the heat on my face and knees. I took another sip of coffee. Placing the book on my lap, I closed my eyes and tried to remember a moment when I had been that content.

CHAPTER 43

Out of consideration for others on the bus who wanted to sleep, I only pulled back the heavy curtains on the window enough to peek through at the scenery. The colours appeared otherworldly, like the cover of a science fiction novel by C.S. Lewis. The setting sun lit the mountains with a rosy hue, while blue shadows smoothed over the otherwise jagged peaks. Green tussocks and round weeds polka-dotted the plains. Brown houses of mud and brick rose from the earth.

We rolled past a distinct outcrop that I recognized from tourist posters in hotel lobbies. Eagle Mountain. It looked like a bird of prey with its wings partially spread, perched atop a kill.

This would be a perfect motorcycle ride, I thought, dearly missing the Oscillator. I shifted in my seat, trying to find a position to alleviate the discomfort in my back. Crossing my legs helped, but only momentarily, and every time I moved them I bumped the seat of the person in front of me. With all the shuffling around, I risked irritating the young man seated next to me as well, although he seemed preoccupied. I never looked at him to verify, but I'm fairly certain he was sobbing.

Man, I hate buses, I thought. If I had my bike I could pull over for a rest, maybe even set up camp in the desert. The more I thought about this, the more claustrophobic I became. It was the lack of control as much as the confined spaces that bothered me.

I closed my eyes and thought back to one of my favourite rides with the Oscillator, earlier in the trip. On that day, the air cooled on the steep climb to Wurzenpass, a high mountain link between Austria and Slovenia, but the sky remained brilliant blue. I honked at dairy cows grazing in the fields and they clanged their cowbells in reply. A ribbon of perfect asphalt dipped in and out of a shady deciduous forest as it rose ever higher, until I reached conifer country at the crest of the pass.

The sun illuminated blue snow-capped mountains with their golden forests as I descended into Slovenia. A stroke of green painted the valley below. An old hymn I had learned as a boy wedged itself into my brain and remained there for the duration of the mountainous ride. "How Great Thou Art" seemed a fitting soundtrack on this stretch, but it got inexplicably replaced in the valley by the Kansas anthem "Carry On Wayward Son."

Cobblestone switchbacks interrupted smooth blacktop, folding in on themselves, forcing me to crawl around the curves at twenty kilometres per hour. Down the mountain, the road opened up to follow a turquoise stream. When the road ran through a village, it only just squeezed between the buildings that defined its margin. Most of the buildings had shed their smooth plaster coatings to expose walls of stone or brick.

I rode on as the shadows got longer. I kept moving to postpone the inevitable. You see, it's easy to ride in foreign countries; it's the stopping that's hard. Really, I hate the hassle of it all – dealing with a language barrier, looking at rooms, unloading gear, maintaining the bike. Sometimes I wish the ride would never end. So even as dusk approached

I kept riding, lost in thought and still humming "Carry On Wayward Son."

Now, crammed into a bus seat, I wished the ride would end immediately. The sun had gone now and there was nothing more to see outside. The bus had rumbled along for hours already, and we still had hours left to go. I put on my headlamp and struggled to remove *A Farewell to Arms* from my bag without creating too much commotion. In the darkness I could hear the man next to me. He was definitely crying.

The bus station in Shiraz has tall palm trees, smooth tile paths, and metal awnings for shelter, but it was dark and I took little notice. People drained out of the bus and disappeared into waiting vehicles, leaving me alone in the black parking lot to search for a taxi. One driver wanted too much money for a ride, but he refused to lower his price. When he left, only one taxi remained. The old man accepted my offer right away and, together with his partner, a young man in a grey jacket, we climbed over a short fence to reach his car.

I squeezed into the front as the old man took his place behind the wheel. Broken springs in the seat forced me to sit lopsidedly, and I had to cock my head to keep it from pressing against the clear plastic liner on the ceiling. My knees bumped against the glove compartment. The young man sat in the back, arguing with the driver over how to find the hotel I wanted.

We idled along a wide street lined with boxy office buildings. The driver stopped often to ask for directions, shouting to pedestrians through my open window. He got out once or twice to limp a few paces down narrow side streets before we eventually found the place at the end of another unlit street. I paid the driver and went inside, where I was shown a room with flaking paint and three dirty beds, each sagging under its own weight. A bare electric bulb hung from the ceiling. The bulb struggled against an oppressive darkness, but only a small part of its light made it through the dusty glass. Perhaps if I had arrived in the light of day I would have checked in, but the room felt sinister now.

It started to rain as I stepped outside. I found one more depressing hotel before stumbling upon an option listed in my guidebook.

Contrary to the guidebook write-up, the staff did not speak English and they were not friendly. The room, however, was clean and I could afford it. I paid ten dollars for the use of a bed and small table. The shower and toilet were down the hall.

Throwing off my wet clothes, I crawled beneath the covers, where I lay awake shivering. I missed the girl that I had left behind in Canada. Our relationship had been on rocky ground before I left and, obviously, it remained that way while I travelled, but I missed her now. Outside it started to pour.

It was not the first time on the trip that I went to bed feeling sorry for myself because I was lonely. For me, it seemed to happen following a particularly unpleasant moment, like here in Shiraz, or for whatever reason following a wonderful day, like the one I had early on in Austria.

The road twisted through the hills over a carpet of oak and maple leaves in the forest that day. Fog thick enough to dampen my boots hung in the air, but I remained warm and dry. Perhaps I should have stopped for pictures, but I felt the pull of momentum. To pause would have interrupted the ride, tainting the moment somehow. In that instant, the rush of the world passing beneath my wheels, curve after curve, far outweighed the desire to make it stand still for my camera.

We broke through the forest, the Oscillator and I, into

a picture postcard of cornfields and pastureland. Farmyards blended into the landscape, their barns finished with white plaster bases and weathered planks on the upper sides. Homes had window shutters and balconies of billowing flowers.

Bypassing Munich, I turned east, riding towards the Alps on the blue horizon. Rather than cut a swath through the woods, builders had allowed groves of trees to remain as the road curved to go around them. As I crossed into Austria, the landscape became more rugged at higher elevations while remaining soft and round in the valleys.

I continued east towards Schladming, a village nestled in a steep valley, where I would spend the night. Everything looked impossibly beautiful, all aglow in the warm light of late afternoon.

Schladming is the kind of European town you'd expect to see pictured on a box of chocolates. When I arrived, I navigated through with ease. Ten years earlier I had spent one of the best summers of my life here, at a light mountaineering school. Memories of that summer came flooding back as I rolled through streets lined with shops and neatly trimmed hedges. I was young here. It was in Schladming that I met some of my dearest friends. It was here that I first fell in love. She was a cute blonde girl from Ontario with the same ideology as me. That was important back then, and it was no coincidence, either. After all, we were at a Christian mountaineering school.

After finding a room and securing the bike, I had dinner on the patio of a familiar restaurant. I had eaten there before, years ago, but never alone. Echoes of laughter to forgotten jokes rang in my head, and the lump in my throat made it difficult for me to swallow my Wiener schnitzel. The nostalgia was overpowering. I nearly cried that night. My melancholy had no chance against a few glasses of Schladminger beer. Also, it didn't help that the restaurant stereo serenaded me with the Bangles' "Eternal Flame."

You might say that an eternal flame burns in my heart for Schladming, but dimly now – the intangible qualities of young companionship and fresh experiences had long ago fled the scene. In the same way that raising a camera to your eye can rob a landscape of its magic, returning to a location can taint a memory with imperfection.

I plodded back to my *gasthaus* in the dark. Perhaps I'd had a few too many Schladmingers that night because, when I awoke in the morning, I discovered a dozen photos on my camera of a simple street sign that read "Ausfahrten."

But there was no beer to lift my spirits here in Shiraz, and no funny street signs. There was only a dirty hotel room on a dark street, and the rain.

A fine road in Slovenia.

Somewhere along the Croatian coast, near Zadar.

Street food, Croatia.

A rundown truck and red earth in Albania,
near the border with Macedonia.

Blue Mosque, Istanbul, Turkey.

Coloured lamps, Grand Bazaar, Istanbul, Turkey.

Men fishing from upper deck of the
Galata Bridge, Istanbul, Turkey.

Fish pulled up from the Bosporus Strait, Istanbul, Turkey.

Playing backgammon with Chikako, Istanbul, Turkey.

Enjoying a beer with German friend Dirk, Istanbul, Turkey.

Sharing a cup of tea with Ebo (centre)
and his two employees, Turkey.

Political demonstration, Ankara, Turkey.

Dust storm between Ar-Raqqah and Deir ez-Zur, Syria.

Near Palmyra, Syria.

KLR650 air filter after the sandstorm, Palmyra, Syria.

A freshly cleaned KLR650 air filter.

The citadel, Aleppo, Syria.

The author and the Oscillator riding the
Great Colonnade at Palmyra, Syria

Krak des Chevaliers, Syria.

Umayyad Mosque, Damascus, Syria.

A friendly crowd presses around the
Oscillator in Deir Hafer, Syria.

Bassam (left) and the author in Deir Hafer, Syria.

Rubbish Mountain, a twenty-metre-high pile of refuse
on the shores of the Mediterranean, Sidon, Lebanon.

An old castle, Sidon, Lebanon.

Cheap rooftop accommodations in Beirut, Lebanon.

The view from a rooftop bedroom, Beirut, Lebanon.

Damage from the 2006 Summer War with Israel
in Haret Hreik, a suburb of Beirut, Lebanon.

Damage from the 2006 Summer War with Israel
in Haret Hreik, a suburb of Beirut, Lebanon.

UN naval personnel march to the top of Our
Lady of Lebanon, near Jounieh, Lebanon.

Image of Hezbollah leader Hassan Nasrallah,
behind decommissioned tank, southern Lebanon.

Baalbek, Lebanon.

A failed attempt to ride a snowy mountain pass, Lebanon.

Billboard near the entrance to
Souq al-Hamidiyya, Damascus, Syria.

The author with his long-overdue Iranian visa, Damascus, Syria.

Friendly local girls in Imam Khomeini Square, Esfahan, Iran.

One of Esfahan's famous bridges, Esfahan, Iran.

Atop the Amir Chakhmaq Complex in Yazd, Iran.

A mosque in Yazd, Iran.

Alexandre (left) and Benoît (right)
at the Tower of Silence, near Yazd, Iran.

A local farmer harvesting turnips and other root vegetables near Yazd, Iran.

A woman walking in the old city of Yazd, Iran.

The Gate of All Nations, Persepolis, Iran.

The Silk Road Hotel, Yazd, Iran.

Christmas at the Silk Road Hotel, Yazd, Iran.

The author smoking narghile, somewhere in the Middle East.

A mosque near the Holy Shrine of Imam Reza, Mashhad, Iran.

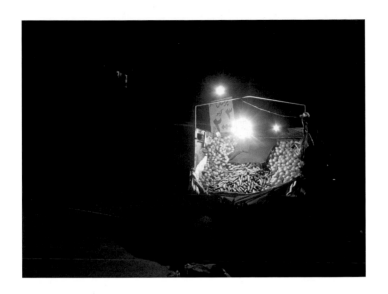

A fruit and vegetable cart in Mashhad, Iran.

A motorcycle courier braves the snow and ice in Tehran, Iran.

A horse in the old city, Damascus, Syria.

Workers abandoned this office tower after discovering
a flawed foundation, Damascus, Syria.

The Oscillator parked in a Syrian hotel
during the author's visit to Iran.

Amanda Lindhout and Travis Woods in
the Old City of Damascus, Syria.

With the Oscillator in Jordan.

CHAPTER 44

Lying in bed the next morning, I could hear the hiss of car tires rolling along wet streets, but the rain had stopped. Down in the dining room, an old man brought me a plate of fried eggs, spongy flatbread, and a frozen packet of butter that I softened up by placing it on the metal lid of the teapot.

After breakfast, I took a walk. I noticed what appeared to be Hezbollah insignia on several buildings. I knew that the Iranian government supported Hezbollah, but I hadn't expected to see such a blatant display of solidarity.

Looking closer, I saw that it was not Hezbollah insignia but the strikingly similar logo of the Iranian Revolutionary Guard. The two organizations had strong connections, as Hezbollah received training from the Revolutionary Guard in the early 1980s. Besides training, the two groups evidently shared a graphic designer.

They shared an overt hatred of Israel and the United States, as well. One had to look no farther than the sidewalk outside of a building displaying the Revolutionary Guard symbol. There, on the ground, they had painted the flags of Israel and the United States so that you had to step on them to enter or exit the building.

Returning to the hotel, I found a man waiting for me in the lobby. He was a thin man with brown skin and eyes so recessed into his head that you could make out the shape of his orbital sockets. He was mostly bald, and what remained of his grey hair he wore cropped close to his skull. On looks alone he would have made an excellent Bond villain in the early films. When he saw me, he removed the cigarette from his lips and stuck out his hand.

"I am Mortazar," he said. Bond villain. "I will drive you to Persepolis." He pronounced it "Purse-police."

Someone in the hotel must have tipped off Mortazar to my presence, because I hadn't set this up.

"I'll think about it," I said in a weak attempt to brush him off. As expected, Mortazar would not accept that answer, but he persisted in a playful way, not obnoxiously, as most unsolicited taxi driver-cum-tour guides would do.

"All right," I conceded. "I will actually consider it. But not today. First I need to extend my visa."

"No problem. I know the man in charge of this. He is my friend."

"Of course he is."

"Really, he is," he insisted. Using the phone in the hotel lobby, Mortazar dialled up Immigration. He dialled the number from memory. After a short discussion, he hung up and said, "We go now. I will help you."

"For how much?" I asked.

"It is nothing," he said with a shrug. "It's for you because you come with me tomorrow."

I shot him a practised look that said both "I promise nothing" and "I'm not an idiot." I use it a lot in the Middle East. Mortazar laughed.

On the drive to the Immigration office Mortazar popped in a cassette tape of oompah music that – and I couldn't have foreseen this – paired well with the crazy traffic. That further cemented him in my mind as the perfect Bond villain. He also caught me up on his background.

Mortazar grew up in Iran, working at a petrochemical plant as a young man. It was a good life, he said, but he lost his job in 1979 when he couldn't play by the new rules set forth by the fledgling Islamic Republic.

"No drinking, no chasing women," he lamented, still incredulous after all these years. "What, are you kidding me?"

He moved to Dubai, where he promptly landed himself in prison for five years for assaulting an Islamic police officer. "I just boxed him one time in the face," Mortazar said, shaking his head. Upon his release, he returned to Iran, where he had been a cab driver ever since.

No longer chasing women or boxing Islamic police, Mortazar now unleashed his aggression on the motoring public. Cursing at how these idiots drive, he squeezed between parked cars on his right and slow-moving vehicles on his left. Finding himself in the middle of an intersection, locked in a traffic jam that he had just created, Mortazar cursed again before reversing back through the narrow corridor, transmission whining over the sound of duelling accordions.

He sniffed out another route and, through a series of increasingly daring manoeuvres, managed to grind traffic to a halt there, too. In this way, from one Mortazar-induced traffic jam to the next, we flung ourselves towards the Immigration office. If he couldn't bring down the Islamic Republic, at least Mortazar could seriously impede its traffic.

Arriving at Immigration, I stepped into a room where two men in mint-green shirts and dark vests sat opposite each other. A glowering picture of the Ayatollah looked down on us all. The officer on the left, who had a thick moustache, motioned for me to hand over my application. After filling out a form of his own, he sent me six paces across the floor to submit them to his partner. That man smacked the papers with a rubber stamp before pointing me back to the moustache man, who signed the stamp and directed me back across the room, six paces.

Bouncing back and forth like that, I began to identify with the pixelated ball in the video game Pong. When next I handed over my papers I said, just softly, "Boop." The man looked up at me. Then he authorized my extension on the spot.

After breakfast the next day, I climbed back into the taxi with Mortazar and an Australian backpacker. Together we ploughed through traffic in Mortazar's special way en route to the ruins of Persepolis.

Our destination brought to mind a graphic novel by the same name. In *Persepolis,* Marjane Satrapi writes of her youth in Iran and the changes brought on by the Islamic Revolution in 1979. She later recalls the Iran-Iraq war and how the Ayatollah gave young men, boys really, plastic keys to hold as they marched through minefields along the border. The keys, they were told, were the keys to heaven. Their march would begin in an earthly minefield, yes, but it would end at the gates of paradise, which would unlock and open wide for them and their plastic keys. That sounds monstrous, but death of any kind isn't so bad if you really believe in heaven or paradise.

A friend of mine in Canada urged me to bring back one of those keys for him.

"That might be a sensitive subject," I said. "Why do you want a key to heaven anyway?"

"Because I want to go to heaven."

"Yeah, but it's the Islamic one."

"I like to have options."

During my time in Iran, I had only inquired about the

keys on a handful of occasions. I asked Mortazar if he knew anything about them.

"No," he said. "Men came to the schools to recruit volunteers for the war, but I never heard of these keys."

From then on I stopped asking about it. The only people likely to have real knowledge on the subject would be the immediate families of the boys who had received those keys so long ago. They would probably be staunch fundamentalists anyway, reluctant to speak with me on such a personal level, if at all.

Besides all that, just asking about the keys made me uncomfortable.

The parking lot was empty when we arrived. It was a bright day without a trace of cloud in the pale sky, but there was also a cold wind that whipped down from the brown, rocky slopes above us. Mortazar produced a thermos of hot water and a jar of Nescafé from the trunk of his car, and we sheltered in the lee of his vehicle to warm ourselves.

Persepolis was once a grand city within the Achaemenid Empire. Darius the Great began work on the city around 518 BCE, and his successors stamped their mark on it through various additions over the next 150 years. It was probably only occupied seasonally, and some scholars think it was a secret city, because there is little mention of it in ancient documents. Alexander the Great burned it down in 330 BCE, but rows of delicate reliefs, columns and stone stairways remain to bear witness to a former glory. It's in good shape now, as ruins go, thanks to the fact that it was lost to history for hundreds of years, only excavated from beneath mounds of earth as recently as the 1930s.

Ascending the Grand Stairway, I approached the Gate of All Nations, or Xerxes Gateway. Two stone carvings of bulls with human heads stood on either side of the gate, facing out towards anyone who dared enter. They reminded me very much of the Golden Sphinxes that guard the Riddle Gate in the old movie version of *The Neverending Story*. In that tale, the two statues face each other while searching the hearts of anyone who wishes to pass. Those who lack a sense of self-worth receive deadly blasts from the shining eyes of each Sphinx.

If that were the case here at the Gate of All Nations, I might be struck down. In fact, I did keep an eye on the stone eyes of each beast for any sign that they would open. The statues each wore a tall hat and a long, neatly squared-off beard. According to the guidebook, the gate bore an inscription in cuneiform that read, "I am Xerxes, Great King, King of kings, King of lands, King of many races … son of Darius the King, the Achaemenid … Many other beautiful things were constructed in Persia. I constructed them and my father constructed them." According to that inscription, at least King Xerxes himself would have had no problems passing through the Sphinxes at the Riddle Gate.

I snickered a little bit. Even though we couldn't be more different, I liked King Xerxes. That was my stage name in college while drumming for the wildly popular heavy metal band the Zygorthian Chronicles. (When I say "wildly popular," I am citing opinions within the band itself.) Although a consensual agreement cannot be made even among band members regarding how many albums we produced, our greatest hits were "Herbicide" and "Put the 'C' Back in Rap."

But I digress. The point is, every time I passed a monument built by or dedicated to King Xerxes, I smiled and hummed a few bars of "Put the 'C' Back in Rap."

If it hadn't been so easy to extend my visa, I would have let it expire just so that I had an excuse to fly back to the Oscillator.

I never recovered from my first dark impressions of Shiraz and, although I had a good day visiting Persepolis and the tomb of King Xerxes, carved like a Greek cross into a sheer mountain face, I still hated the city. Certainly the weather didn't help. Overcast skies, intermittent rain, and a biting wind kept me chained to the hotel.

Also, on this particular day, I longed for the comfort of friends and family. Try as I might to push these desires from my mind, to think of it as just another day on the road, I wanted to see decorations and lights. I wanted church bells and music. It was Christmas Eve, but everywhere I looked in Shiraz I only saw grey.

I stopped in at a travel agency to inquire about flights to the south of Iran. After a few weeks in the country I had a better feel for how massive it was and, thinking of the miserable bus journey that brought me to Shiraz, I wanted to fly. Besides, flights in Iran were cheap.

The agent wore a tight wrap to cover her hair, and a loose covering over that to frame her face and accentuate her chocolate-coloured eyes. When she fixed those eyes on me it made me stammer to the point where I asked for a private plane.

"You want a private plane?" she said, leaning closer with, I think, a mischievous smile.

Yes, if that would impress you, I thought. Actually, I just corrected myself and asked about regular commercial flights. She checked her computer. To Bandar-e-Abbas, a port city on the Strait of Hormuz in the Persian Gulf, all flights were full. No matter. I had only planned to visit Bandar to ship across to the United Arab Emirates with my motorcycle. Now that I thought about it, without the Oscillator I had no reason to go.

"Can you check for Bushehr?" I asked.

Another city on the shores of the Persian Gulf, Bushehr had an old city of some interest, but really I wanted to go because Bushehr had gained a lot of international attention of late. It is the site of one of Iran's controversial nuclear power plants. Although not yet operational, it had recently received shipments of fuel from Russia.

The travel agent tapped "Bushehr" into the computer. "All full," she said. "The bus is full, too."

Just as well. Was I expecting a tour of the plant? No. Would I hop the fence like I had in Lebanon to see Rubbish Mountain? The nuclear plant probably has a better fence.

"If you leave in two days," she continued, "then I could book you a seat to either destination."

Through the window I could see ghosts of fog lifting from the pavement as the sun warmed the wet streets. It looked like a nice day after all. Perhaps if I stayed I could pay my respects at the grave of Zahra Kazemi. I knew that she was buried in Shiraz, but I had no idea if it would be easy to find her tomb.

Beyond that, Shiraz had other things to offer. Everyone said so. It had gardens, mosques, tombs of poets. It had interesting places to eat. It had culture.

"What about Yazd?" I said at last. "Can you put me on a bus today?"

"There is just one seat left," she said.

"Book it."

Three hours later, I boarded a white Volvo bus with a mural of a praying woman on the back. In English it read, "Hope to God."

I might not share Christmas with family, I thought, but at least I'll be with other travellers. That's a sort of family. And the Silk Road Hotel has a Christmas tree.

CHAPTER 45

I spent Christmas Day in the courtyard of the Silk Road Hotel with other travellers, reading, writing in our journals, laughing. Late in the afternoon, I summoned the energy to explore another covered souk with vaulted ceilings and bustling shops in the old city. There I bumped into Christian, an Austrian traveller I had met on the bus from Shiraz.

We strolled over to the Amir Chakhmaq Complex, a three-storey structure with two tall towers, blue tiles, and dozens of arching alcoves. There we embarked on a dizzying ascent of brick stairs that spun us steeply through one of the towers to the top for a clear view of Yazd. The sky curved above us like an overturned cereal bowl, with faint streaks of cloudy milk pooling along the rim of the horizon. The city spread out like a wheat field before the harvest, changing colours with the setting sun but never far away from golden brown, while the domes and minarets of various mosques stood out like emeralds in the field, as if God were the only one who bothered painting his house every spring.

There were *badgirs*, or wind towers, that jutted up from behind the walls of many homes. The brown rectangular structures had vertical slits in them for collecting outside air. Through a series of flues, the towers forced air down to cool over an underground water source before circulating through the home. They peppered the skyline and would have dominated the cityscape if not for the glimmering mosques.

Looking down, we watched workers preparing the grounds for an upcoming visit from Ayatollah Khamenei, who would address the crowd from this very building in a few days.

With sunlight fading, Christian and I returned to the Silk Road Hotel. One of the guests had organized a communal meal, and we didn't want to miss it. That same guest had had the foresight to load Christmas music onto his iPod before leaving home, which he then piped through the hotel sound system.

The courtyard sparkled with coloured lights and dozens of candles as they glinted off tinsel and foil garlands. The tables had been pushed together and covered with a red cloth to create one large dining area with a centrepiece of fruit, nuts and candy arranged around a white candle.

When it was time, vagabonds from nearly every continent gathered around the table to share a meal. Just before we ate, I asked if someone would like to say grace. A young Italian in a hemp poncho jumped up on his chair. Camillo pronounced blessings on us all in Latin, crossing himself and the table in mock homage to Catholic liturgy. Everyone laughed. Someone shouted "Pope Camillo!" After that, there was no way a person could transition into any kind of meaningful prayer.

The meal lasted for hours. Long after we had finished eating, we lingered at the table ordering rounds of Coke, ice cream, coffee, and tea. At last, fully impaired by every sort of stimulant still permissible within the Islamic Republic – caffeine, sugar, nicotine – we stayed up listening to Christmas music, the hiss of the gas heater, and the flapping of the tarpaulin overhead as the wind snapped at it. As far as Christmases on the road go, I could have wanted nothing more – nothing more, that is, except for someone to have said grace.

CHAPTER 46

Days later, I awoke on the top berth of a Pullman just as the train rolled into the station at Mashhad. Once again, I had pried myself free of Yazd even though I had excuses to stay. If I had waited another two days, I could have seen Ayatollah Khamenei as he addressed the crowd from the Amir Chakhmaq Complex.

It was just another snap decision that brought me to Mashhad. Other travellers at the Silk Road had told me about the city, located in the northeast corner of Iran, about one hundred kilometres from the border with Turkmenistan. They told me that the Holy Shrine of Imam Reza, located in Mashhad, was the holiest site in the entire nation. For that reason alone, I decided to visit.

Still groggy from a restless night in the hot sleeper car, I stepped into the flow of passengers pouring down the aisle, spilling out into the stinging cold outside the train. The stream of people carried me towards the station, where a man stood at the entrance, burning incense that looked like a kids' sugar cereal in a shallow dish.

After a short taxi ride I opened the door to my hotel room. The room had two beds, a window opening onto a small balcony, and a private bathroom that reeked so powerfully of stagnant water that I had to skip in and out while holding my breath. That last detail explained why it only cost ten dollars per night. Otherwise, everything was perfect.

Outside, a pale sun bleached away colour from the city just as it had done in Esfahan, but it did nothing to warm the air. As long as I kept moving I could stay warm. In fact, a brisk walk in direct sunlight could produce perspiration on my brow beneath my black toque. As soon as I slowed my pace or lingered in the shade, I began to shiver. I had stepped out to find the Shrine that afternoon, and I found it at last on the very boundary of what I considered a reasonable walking distance from the hotel.

Leaving my pack with an attendant near the door, I approached a security checkpoint where several men stood guard over the entrance. Following a light patdown, they waved me through into a vast courtyard of polished stone. I managed a few steps before halting dead in my tracks.

In every direction, there stood an architectural marvel silently defying me to assign it only one superlative in my notebook. Colossal minarets loomed over the expansive compound along the outer wall, and the minarets of a more modest size shone with gilded brilliance as if to mentor the sun.

After staring for a few seconds, I began walking again, slowly, trying to take it all in. Men burning incense. Women in chadors. A mother and daughter walked together; the girl, perhaps four years old, wore a full niqab like her mom. There were men in white turbans and brown robes that flowed as they walked. There were others with black turbans, an indication that they were descended from the Prophet Mohammed himself. Many men wore beards and some had prayer bumps on their foreheads: patches of discoloured skin from years of touching down to prayer mats.

I hoped to observe everything without drawing too much attention to myself. This was a holy site after all, not a tourist attraction. Really, I did not belong there. Much of the compound was simply off-limits to non-Muslims. I knew that from speaking with travellers, some of whom warned that a trip to Mashhad would be a waste of time with all the restrictions. My abridged guidebook confirmed these reports, but only in a cursory way. It failed to identify the places that I, an infidel, should avoid.

As it turns out, infidels should avoid everything. Being a non-Muslim, I was to report immediately to the tourist office. There, I would be assigned a guide to shepherd me around, limiting my visit to the outer courtyards. That information, however, along with stern warnings to not even attempt entering the mosques – certainly not the Shrine itself – only came to my attention long after I had left Mashhad when I read it in the proper guidebook that I had sent home from Syria. The problem, said the guidebook, was not a lack of faith on my part but that, as an unbeliever, I would not have performed the ritualistic purification required, nor would I have taken the time to prepare my heart for such an important pilgrimage.

Continuing along on my own, I passed through gaping archways of intricate blue-and-yellow tile, wandering deeper into the compound and more intimate spaces. The turquoise dome that capped the Great Mosque of Gohar Shad, with its ring of decorative tile and yellow calligraphy, towered over another monumental archway before a smaller courtyard covered with red carpet. That dome might have dominated the skyline on the merit of its size, except that it sat opposite another feature … smaller, but far more majestic.

There, settled between two glistening minarets, stood the resplendent golden dome that marked the Shrine of

Imam Reza. Even amidst all the grandeur of the surrounding architecture, it stood out like a diamond ring on a velvet pillow. It rose into an elegant cylinder before tapering off to a point, making other domes appear homely by comparison. A blue band with golden Arabic script wrapped around it like a satin sash, while a green flag swayed on top like a silk ribbon in the hair of a beautiful maiden.

At this point, I did stop to stare. I could not help it.

Though it still glinted off the dome in a dazzling display, by now the sun had dropped too low in the sky to offer any of its rays to the ground. Clutching elbows tight to my chest, I blew into my hands to keep them warm. There was so much more I wanted to see, but the cold made it difficult to appreciate. Maybe I could just find some place to warm up.

A throng of people gathered beneath the golden dome at the entrance, removing their shoes before stepping inside. I joined them. Kneeling down at the edge of the crowd, I untied my boots and placed them in a clear plastic bag. I knew that I would be barred from entering the Shrine itself, but no one seemed to have any objections to my presence thus far.

Just the same, I avoided eye contact with people, especially the ushers, or guards. One could identify them by the feather dusters they carried on the end of long, slender poles. With these, they could reach over shoulders in the crowd and tap an individual on the head if they needed to get his attention.

I didn't sneak in, exactly, but I did join a particularly large rush of people as they made their way through the doors. Also, I timed my entrance with the pacing of the usher as he turned to walk in the other direction.

Until then, I must have done a fair job of blending into the crowd, but if anyone had looked into my face the moment I stepped through that door, they would have found there such an expression of awed bewilderment as to single me out instantly. Keeping pace with the flow of men in front of me, I moved through a cavernous mosque tiled to the ceiling with sparkling mirrors – thousands of them. Hundreds of thousands. It seemed as if all the geometric designs of tile work in other mosques were here recreated with mirrors reflecting at different angles. I had crawled into the largest chandelier in the universe, or a disco ball with mirrors on the inside.

At first blush, that description sounds tacky. "A bunch of mirrored tiles? Didn't they decorate bathrooms like that in the sixties?" Not like this. No. It was absolutely over the top. With such an overwhelming display of visuals to drink in, I only managed to retain a few images in my mind as I passed through the building. Large chandeliers. Marble floors. A great mass of worshippers praying, reading from the Quran. Weeping.

Men touched wooden doors as they passed through before touching their chests. They fingered a smooth silver grate, holding onto it reverentially. So did I. But I never stopped for long. That would make me look conspicuous – or worse, someone might try to speak with me. I didn't know if this building was off limits to non-Muslims before I entered, but now I felt certain that it was. The Holy Shrine must be very near, I thought. Frankly, I did not want to see it. Not now. After all, I was an imposter.

I just wanted to get out.

Trying to look as though I had purpose, I kept moving like I had somewhere to go and I knew how to get there. In this manner, I found the exit, stepping out through doors beneath an archway leafed to the tip with gold.

Back in the cold air near the shining dome, I stooped to lace up my boots. My head buzzed from the effort of trying to process all that I had seen. It was too much. I wandered the courtyard in a fog, dismissing from my memory nearly everything I saw the moment I looked away.

I vaguely remembered people weeping, still bitterly mourning the death of their fallen spiritual leader, which occurred centuries ago. Then something grabbed my full attention. I stood agape for at least the third time that day, blinking several times before the image registered in my mind.

I've seen too much, I thought. *My head is broken.*

There, cooing at my feet, stood a real dove with purple plumage. Bright purple. When it flew away, I watched it go. Then I decided that I had better return to the hotel.

CHAPTER 47

Mashhad has nothing to offer the visitor as far as attractions go. It is a sprawling city of nearly three million people with boxy buildings and a hazy brown sky. Most people come to pay their respects to Imam Reza at the Shrine, and then they leave.

I decided to look around anyway. Along major roads near the Shrine complex, I noticed many shops selling jars of red saffron. Farther down there was a bakery where a team of men tossed dough into a fire oven, pulling out hot discs of bread moments later.

Dozens of portrait studios lined the streets as well. Here, one could pose for a photo and have that photo superimposed onto any backdrop. Smiling Iranian families stood before images such as waterfalls, bright flowers, or strangely disproportionate animals like giant swans and tiny deer. Religious themes were the most popular, however. People often chose the Holy Shrine of Imam Reza or the Great Mosque, for example.

Along the way, I stepped into a narrow restaurant, a hole in the wall slotted between two larger shops. As the place had no menus, I pointed to what the man next to me was eating. The waiter returned with a plate of flatbread; a slender cast-iron bowl, piping hot; and a few accessories, namely an empty bowl and a heavy mallet. It all looked like so much fun, but I didn't know what to do. With furtive glances, I observed the man beside me. He tore off a piece of bread to use as a pot holder on the cast-iron vessel. From there he poured out a thin orange broth into the bowl to eat with a spoon, tossing in chunks of bread to give it substance.

Next came the mallet. It was a pestle, really, with a flat, round head used to smash the remaining ingredients in the cast-iron pot all to mush. First I looked inside. I could not identify everything, but there was a hunk of white fat, some stringy meat, a chunk of potato, chickpeas, and possibly corn. After giving it all a solid beating, I scooped it into the silver bowl to eat like hummus with the remaining bread.

I found out later that the dish is called *abgoosht*. The stuff I had wasn't particularly tasty, but it was filling. With a pot of tea and a can of Coke, the bill came to two dollars.

After paying, I gathered my things to leave. That's when I met Mahdi.

"Where are you from?" he asked, just as I was about to step outside.

Turning around, I saw a diminutive man with a trim beard. He wore crisp attire, all black from his scarf down to shiny shoes.

"Are you Christian?" he said.

There's that question again. I nodded before moving on to more small talk. When he asked what I thought of Mashhad, I told him it was nice.

"But," I said, "it's a shame that I can't visit the Shrine."

Mahdi flinched as if I had reached out to poke him in the face with a stick.

"What? Why not?"

"Well, because I'm not a Muslim."

"Oh, but you have to see it," he replied. "It's the very reason people come to Mashhad. If you go with me, I think you can see it."

He scrawled a phone number on a piece of paper, urging me to call him sometime over the next few days.

"Well, why don't we go later tonight?" I said. "We could meet right back here."

Mahdi agreed.

Together Mahdi and I walked briskly to the Shrine complex, hurrying along in an effort to get out of the biting wind. He was still dressed in black, his long overcoat buttoned all the way up to his neatly wrapped scarf. He was dressed for mourning, I would soon learn. Mahdi was devout and, with his black clothing, he was already preparing for Ashura (although it had not yet begun).

Ashura is a ten-day commemoration of what happened in Karbala in 680 CE, when Mohammed's grandson Hussein, son of Ali, was sold out and killed along with his hopelessly outnumbered warrior companions. Just fifty years after Mohammed's natural death, this slaughter was the final, irreparable rift that splits the Shia and Sunni today. The Shia still manage to weep real tears for Hussein, and in some of their more visual displays of mourning, they will beat their chests and even cut themselves, allowing blood to flow down their faces.

"Every day is Ashura," they say, "and every land is Karbala."

The way Mahdi dressed had more than just symbolic meaning that day. The way he wrapped up in the cold, that's what made our mission possible. It meant that other men would be bundled up, too. The other day I had noticed many of them wearing woollen hats, just like mine – only mine disguised hair that was much too long, too curly, and too blond to be discreet.

If I had really wanted to slip in unnoticed, I should have done something about my beard. Looking around, I noticed that most men were clean-shaven. Those who weren't had moustaches or short beards, and they were always black. Mine came in quite red with hints of grey. By this time on the journey, I had let the thing get all long and scruffy. There was no hiding behind it now. It looked less like a blanket of anonymity on my face than it did a calico cat.

At any rate my blue eyes gave me away, but what could I do about that? I just hoped that, with Mahdi's help, I would look like I belonged.

Passing through security, Mahdi paused in front of a large sign with rows of text.

"What does it say?" I asked.

"It's just a sign of respect to read it," he replied. "Here we are asking permission to enter."

"Oh," I said, pretending to read along. "Asking who for permission?"

"It's better if you don't speak."

I nodded. People should tell me that more often.

From then on, whenever we passed before the scrutiny of a guard, Mahdi turned to me and spoke Farsi. It was my job to act like I was listening.

Moving through the outer courtyards, Mahdi explained some finer points of Islam to me, as he understood them.

"There are twelve imams," he said. "Eleven died, but the twelfth was taken away by God before he died. He is still alive, you understand? He will return one day." This is where Mahdi got his name. That twelfth imam, the one spirited away by God, the one who will return to rule before Judgement Day and who will rid the world of wrongdoing, that imam was named Muhammed al-Mahdi.

Though I listened respectfully, when Mahdi said that this imam didn't die I remember thinking, "That sounds kind of crazy." I'm sure that my expression never changed, but Mahdi must have seen the doubt in my eyes, because next he said, "With Jesus. The twelfth imam will return with Jesus. He is our prophet too."

Point taken. What's crazier, to believe that Mahdi didn't die and will come back, or that Jesus did die, but got back up and will come back? Besides, we have our prophets in the Bible who never died as well. It is always easier to look critically at a belief system when it belongs to someone else. Many of these stories ranked about the same on the Scale of Plausibility.

I wondered, not for the first time, whether the faint hope to which I clung only remained because I had been dropped into a certain faith at birth, placated with simple answers before I could form complex questions. I could have replied to Mahdi with the very words of a character from *Perelandra*, by C.S. Lewis: "'I get the idea,' said Ransom, 'that the account a man gives of the universe, or of any other building, depends very much on where he is standing.'"

I looked up. Gargantuan minarets stood out against the night sky, glowing like ghostly fingers pointing out into black, infinite space. From where I was standing, my account of the universe needed to shift if it was to include God.

"When will the imam and Jesus return?" I asked Mahdi.

"When the world is filled with evil," he said. "When people have tried many other ways to make things right and failed."

"So ... any time now."

Mahdi smiled. "Inshallah," he said. God willing.

At the entrance to another mosque, Mahdi and I placed our shoes in plastic bags to carry. This building, like so much of the complex both inside and out, was under construction. Like other mosques, it had soft red carpet on the floor and high, domed ceilings. The walls were white for now, but workers were tiling them with mirrors just like the Shrine of Imam Reza.

Once inside, we kept quiet. Through a series of rooms and corridors, he led me back into the building containing the Holy Shrine. Following Mahdi's example, I touched doors, I touched my heart. Sometimes I kissed my hand and touched the doors.

"We don't have to do this," said Mahdi in a low voice, anticipating my questions. "Touching the doors ... it's not a rule. It's just that we love the imam so much, you see."

Finally we came to the entrance of the Shrine itself. I was right. I had passed very near this space the day before. I could have made it here on my own, but it was better with a companion.

A man in front of us knelt to kiss the marble doorsill. Mahdi did not kneel, but he did pause. He bowed and touched his head. He touched golden doors, protected now behind glass. Stepping to the entryway before the Shrine, I could see why we took a moment to ready ourselves. With its towering ceiling, the room beamed with heavenly glory. In the middle stood the tall rectangular Shrine, its silver lattice polished by the tender caresses of innumerable adoring hands. Higher up, too high for people to reach, the walls appeared lacklustre, but only by comparison. They shone as well, further adorned with gold. Green velvet on top, chandeliers hanging from long golden chains, mirrors and coloured tiles. Everything seemed to have a luminescence of its own except for us, the mass of people below. Mainly dressed in black, we appeared as shadowy creatures with no glory but that which reflected off us from other sources.

A murmur filled the room as everyone prayed out loud, or stood back to read from the Quran. Now and again, someone would raise his voice above the others, speaking for everyone to hear. When this happened, the crowd responded like a Pentecostal congregation shouting "Amen!" at a charismatic preacher.

As for me, I stood in wonder against a back wall with Mahdi at my side. Men jammed together as they jostled for position, shuffling forward on the marble floor to press up against the Shrine. Here they offered prayers, tied green ribbons to the silver lattice, or shoved wadded-up money through the holes. If a man could not reach the Shrine, he sometimes passed the money forward through the crowd.

"Here," said Mahdi, "you can ask whatever you want and it will be given to you."

That sounded familiar. While I listened, my eyes darted around the room, trying to focus on something but finding too much detail to settle anywhere.

"I have seen it," said Mahdi. "I have seen people healed. There is a way to look in at the Shrine from outside, I will show you later. People are healed there."

"But, not everyone gets healed, right?" I said, thinking about my back. That would be too easy.

"No," Mahdi conceded. "First you must have a special relationship with the imam."

That sounded familiar, too.

Finally, we entered the flow of people pushing their way towards the Shrine. The crowd carried us near the lattice and spit us out another archway as we turned to back away. Everyone did this, keeping their eyes on the Shrine as long as possible, touching their heads, touching their hearts, some of them crying.

We ended up in an adjacent room of mirrors and marble. Mahdi made to leave, but I hesitated. Just like during my first visit to this building, I felt overwhelmed. My mind spun with the effort of trying to take in some detail of the Shrine, only to realize that I had already forgotten what it looked like. There was just too much to see, too much to comprehend. I could stand there for a lifetime and never grasp it all. New images pushed old ones from my memory at an alarming rate. I couldn't simply pull out my notebook, either. Not here. That would draw attention. And even if I ran straight back to my hotel to write everything down, it would be like trying to describe all the shapes I had seen in a kaleidoscope.

At the door, I paused, glancing over my shoulder.

"Do you want to go back in?" asked Mahdi.

I nodded. Perhaps the universe would shift tonight.

I wanted to return to see the Shrine, and the room, and the lights, and the mirrors. More than that, I wanted to see people worship. There, pressed against the Holy Shrine, that is what they did. With unrivalled adoration, thousands of miles from where my own path began, men stood calling out to the God of Abraham. They used a different name for him than I was used to. They approached him by a different channel, but they did so faithfully, with all earnestness.

If God listens, then I can only hope that he will respond to a man who really seeks him, crying out for answers, for understanding. And there, in that building, I saw men beseech God with undeniable sincerity. There, in that building, God replied. Didn't he? Mahdi believed so. Except there, God answered with a different voice than the one we claim to hear in the West. That made no sense. Were we not also sincere?

Mahdi lifted a Quran from a shelf before returning to the Shrine. We stood back against the wall again. While he read out loud, I kept still, doing my best to listen to a language that I could not understand. Soon his voice faded. I found myself alone with my thoughts.

Years ago I had stopped praying. Not entirely, I confess.

Nearly every day, in fact, I still directed some words towards God while walking around, or while riding my motorcycle, but I stopped setting aside the time. Now the remarks often consisted of one or two sentences, quickly formed and forgotten.

I remember the day that change took place. Years of struggle led to it, but it happened suddenly. One night, kneeling beside the bed, I felt like a child talking to an imaginary friend. My prayers hit the ceiling and stuck there. That was it.

Here, though, prayers could reach heaven. Angels ascended and descended in this very room, said Mahdi. To me, that seemed like another ridiculous superstition, but it didn't matter. A prayer that I could not stifle welled up within me as though invisible hands reached in to pull it from my chest. Abandoning convention, I sought God – not mine, not theirs or yours. Just God.

My heart unleashed a cry for understanding, for the wisdom to recognize every misconception that I have about the Divine. If God is bigger than I am, if he is bigger than us all, then surely I have more than one misconception. I begged for the courage to abandon everything that is false, no matter how sacred I once held it. I called out for the strength to hang on to every shred of truth, no matter how small. How tragic if, by some miracle, I had grown up with the truth only to abandon it because it seemed too simple, too fanciful or superstitious.

Returning to a fuller awareness of my surroundings, I looked over at Mahdi. He had stopped reading from the Quran to watch me pray.

"This is your imam, too," he said. "There is only one God. So, in a way, everyone is a Muslim. Just those who follow other religions have yet to perfect their faith."

Interesting. Ditto that for every monotheistic religion,

though. He went on to say that no one can visit the Shrine without being invited by the imam. "So, because you are here," he said, "you have been called."

I liked that. I didn't believe it, exactly. It was another exercise in circular reasoning, but it felt good to hear. I was called. Mahdi affirmed my right to be there, but he quickly added, "If you ever want to visit again, you better go with me. Some people see things differently and may not allow you to enter."

As I was still wrapped in layers of warm clothing, the heat in the room became overbearing. Once more, Mahdi and I entered the push of people as we exited the room. This time, the crowd moved me close enough to the Shrine that I could reach out and touch the engravings on the corner. I held the grate for a moment before backing away with Mahdi. Removing my toque, I placed it over my heart. I took it off partly out of respect, but mostly because I was overheating. Several young men noticed this and looked at me, their eyes betraying a look of surprise.

"It's better to keep your hat on," warned Mahdi.

My hair marked me as a tourist, a fact that I resented. I was not a tourist, not at that moment. I had come to find God and to worship. I was a seeker. The imam had called me here, according to Mahdi, and I had answered that call. I prayed just like everyone else: with reverence, in humility and awe. Of course, I was no closer at all to accepting Islam, but to worship within a community ... it felt good.

And God did hear my prayer. He took note. Before I could escape the city of Mashhad, God would steal into my hotel room. He would arrive unannounced late at night and threaten me with death.

CHAPTER 48

The next afternoon I returned to the Holy Shrine. I went alone. Moving confidently through the building, I found that the intensity of the previous night's experience had grown faint. I felt a like a tourist this time, I admit.

Still, I stepped lightly, but I spent more time looking around than I did considering faith. The mirrors only began at about shoulder height. Below that, marble covered the walls. The marble came in all colours, but it was often green, with some white, rose and black pieces arranged in geometric patterns. Without pause, I stepped into the room containing the Shrine, moving straight into the flow of people rather than lingering there. Backing away with my hand on my heart, I found myself in an outer room.

I returned later to the complex to ring in the new year. It struck midnight just as I entered the courtyard of the Great Mosque. As the Islamic new year falls on a different date, no one else noticed.

New Year's Day would be my last in Mashhad. I had booked a flight for Tehran early the following morning. From there I would fly to Damascus for a long-anticipated reunion with the Oscillator. And from there? Well, I had no idea.

On the afternoon of New Year's Day, I visited the Shrine one last time. As I stepped up to the security checkpoint, a guard asked me, "Are you Muslim?"

"Inshallah," I replied.

They all laughed before letting me through without frisking me.

I had no intention of visiting the actual Shrine as I had the day before. I only wanted to see the sunset reflected off the golden dome.

Everything in the Shrine complex that night seemed to dance beneath a dynamic orange sky – every blue and yellow tile, every green flag and red carpet. But the golden dome remained steadfast even in the shifting light of the setting sun. At last the sun burned through silver clouds, reflecting off the marble floor to backlight the crowd with a fiery glow, and then it was gone.

I decided to enter the Great Mosque after all. I noticed new details with every visit. This time it was a few patches of gold mirrors, and mirrored Arabic script on rich blue or green backgrounds.

Then, although I had not intended to visit, I stood before the Holy Shrine once again. Approaching the golden doors, I touched them, but I did not enter the room. I walked right on past. The first visit inspired a real prayer. The second time was neat, but I was a tourist. This time, at that very moment, I had "Rock You Like a Hurricane" by the Scorpions in my head.

CHAPTER 49

Midnight. Stripes of black and orange stretched across the floor from a street light stealing in through slats on the hotel window. Outside, the night was dead. No sound of traffic. No voices. No wind or rain. Only silence. Inside, the faucet drip, drip, dripped in the bathroom. A foul smell of bad air crept in from beneath the door.

I had just about fallen asleep when something forced me to attention – something terrible. Sitting bolt upright in bed, I stared into the shadows like the old man from "The Tell-Tale Heart." No one peering in through a crack in the door. No lantern on a vulture eye. But, like the old man's, my heart beat furiously for fear of death. I sat there, panting like I had just scrambled up from the cellar.

The sand in my hourglass coagulated to the point where it nearly stopped flowing altogether while I sat in the dark, my heart thumping hard against my ribs. *Dear God*, I thought, *what if I die here tonight, so far away from everyone who cares?* Then I wondered if it would really be any different from dying near loved ones. I guessed not.

It was 12:20 a.m. I switched on the light. After what had just happened, I would not be sleeping anytime soon.

Unlike the incident with my rain jacket in Bozüyük, this time the threat to my life was real. My fear, I felt, was justifiable. Right at the moment where I had nearly drifted off to sleep, my heart had fluttered. It struggled to keep time, unnerving me to the point where my eyes snapped open. I lay there taking deep breaths. That helped. My heart soon found its rhythm, but now it pulsed with shallow, rapid beats as if the chambers were filled with air, not blood. A hollow heart.

I needed to calm down, so I whispered apologies in the dark.

I'm sorry. I'm sorry. I'm sorry.

If I did die, those would be my last words. The whispers became softer until I only mouthed the phrase. Finally my lips stopped moving and I only thought it, *I'm sorry*. When I had quieted my mind I teetered on the brink of consciousness, ready once again for sleep. This time, my heart did not flutter.

It stopped.

With a great gasp I sprang to. Adrenaline kicked my heart hard enough to crush it, but it started instead. Thumping now. Sitting up in bed, my chest felt constricted like an invisible band of steel wrapped around me, squeezing tighter and tighter. I struggled to breathe as if through a narrow straw while my heart pounded, faster now, rising until I could feel its pulse in my neck and ears.

It is a frightening thing to be aware of your own heartbeat. Under normal circumstances, you should never notice it. At that moment, I could think of nothing else. Nothing else mattered, just that my heart would keep beating. It fluttered again. Several times it stopped, or seemed to, pounding my ribs from inside each time as it caught its rhythm.

Heart attack.

I was standing in the dark now, afraid for my life. Should I go for help right now? Each heartbeat could be the last.

What if it seized completely, like a motorcycle engine that ran out of oil? I don't know. I could survive it, maybe.

Enduring incredible pain, I'd fight to get downstairs. If I could find someone at the front desk I'd have to communicate my need for a doctor. That part should be easy. Collapsing on the floor should do the trick. I imagined the sound of my skin slapping against the cold tile – the last sound I'd ever hear.

I wished for daylight. That seemed manageable somehow, like I could handle it all right if only my heart stopped beating during the day. But at night ... Hemingway was right: "It is awfully easy to be hard-boiled about everything in the daytime, but at night it is another thing."

It can't be a heart attack, though, I thought. It only came on at the point where I nearly fell asleep, when I was at my most relaxed. No. Not a heart attack.

With the light on, everything seemed much better. I got dressed and sat down with my journal to write, describing what had just happened.

What had happened? Was it God grabbing my attention, or – wait – punishing me for entering the Holy Shrine of Imam Reza without proper preparation? No, of course not. Not that. Why would I even consider such nonsense? The answer to that, at least, was easy: it was dark outside.

What, then? Thinking back, the feeling that I had in my chest, the tightness, the shallow heartbeats and laboured breathing, it all reminded me of something that I had known in the past. Something innocuous. In fact, it never really concerned me at the time because I had understood the source. Except for the most dramatic symptoms, I had gone through this years before after breaking up with a girl. That was it. It reminded me of grief-induced heartache.

When I pieced that together, the steel band around my chest loosened off some, although that still failed to explain the part where I thought my heart had stopped. With the lights on, I nearly convinced myself that I had imagined that bit, but no – something had jolted me awake.

Also, I hadn't broken up with anyone. There should be no sense of loss, no heartache.

I shivered. It was still blackest night outside. One o'clock in the morning now.

Could it be? I thought. *Is this how it feels to break up with God?*

Our relationship had been going that way for some time. By every human measure it was dysfunctional. Just consider how ineffectively we communicated. I stopped speaking because I could never tell if he was listening and, as far as I knew, he never said anything. Or maybe he did speak, but everything could be interpreted in so many ways that it was meaningless.

For example, my heart problems might be a message from God, but what did it mean? Was he telling me to leave Mashhad, or to stay? Should I pick up the Muslim faith, or return to my roots? Or maybe God just wanted me to eat properly and exercise.

So we communicated poorly. Still, an unhealthy relationship differs from none at all. Sometimes, even in a troubled marriage a certain comfort remains. While a divorce may be for the best, it would still dredge up a lot of pain.

At the Holy Shrine I had prayed for the courage to abandon misconceptions about the Divine. What if that was all that I had? What if I had to begin my search all over again? I had watched some of my friends do exactly that. They stepped off the foundation on which they had built their lives. They seemed happy. Most of them chuckled now at how silly they were to have ever believed in a god of any kind. To me that seemed a very brave thing to do. Could I do it, too? Should I? Was it even my choice?

I mean, what if there really is a God, one similar to the one I had once tried to understand? When would he grow weary of my insolence and doubt? At what point would he stop believing in me?

The questions flooded to mind. More and more questions, all very interesting, but all of them unanswerable. At some point I had to make a decision based on incomplete information. That's faith. That did not mean, however, that once the decision was made it should never again be re-evaluated. That's dogma.

In recent years I had been leaning towards the opinion that there was no God, or at very least that God looked radically different from the one I had envisioned. It was like I had told Chikako that night in Istanbul, standing on the bridge over the dark water of the Bosporus. I once claimed to know God. I knew that he existed. I knew that he had communicated to us through an ancient text that contained no flaws.

Then, in time, I met other people who claimed to know things about God as well, things that they had learned from different books. Where their knowledge contradicted mine, they were just wrong. They were reading the wrong book. This is how religious wars get started.

Eventually such arrogance faded, either because I grew older or because I travelled more. Knowledge became belief, and I think I took a small step towards truth at that point. That was a smooth transition. What came next was hard.

With the same skepticism usually reserved for other religions, I began examining my own. For years, I agonized over why I still hoped in God. Perhaps, there in Mashhad, I had my answer. It was fairly basic, actually. Although my mind often told me to walk away, my spirit would not go. My heart argued the case for God, though obviously never with a great deal of sophistication. Look at its tack tonight.

It just stopped. It struck up a strange collaboration between its physical and metaphorical self to get me out of bed and thinking about God.

And it worked. I thought a lot that night, running over the same questions, the same doubts that I had had all along. Of course, no matter how long I stared at the problem, I knew that I would not shed any new light on the matter, not then and there, anyway, alone in that hotel room. I would only unearth the same old fear – fear that God did not exist or, even more frightening, that he did.

In the end, I had to admit that a faint hope in God would last through the night. Already I had made too many rash decisions on this trip, including the decision to embark on a journey to Iran in the first place. Then, when it looked as if I would not reach that goal, I abandoned the guidebook.

Well, I would learn from it. Before stepping off the path, before completely turning away from my original direction in search of God, I would consider it very carefully.

The next time I threw away another guidebook, I needed to be sure.

CHAPTER 50

I waited at the small airport in Mashhad for the better part of a day before they finally cancelled our flight to Tehran due to inclement weather. With the help of Aref and Mahmoud, two English-speaking Iranians who befriended me, I refunded my ticket and booked a night train instead.

The three of us took a cab to Aref's brother's house to wait, where we were served tea and cookies by Aref's sister-in-law. Other travellers told me that they had received countless invitations like this into the homes of local Iranians. That hadn't been my experience, but I learned later that it might have been on account of my thick beard. People could have taken that as a sign that I supported the Iranian regime.

When he returned from work, Aref's brother brought with him black-market whiskey. Leery from my experience with Iranian beer, I refused to get my hopes up right away. I examined the can. There was the first problem, it came in a can. At least the can had no Farsi writing on it, which meant I could hope just a little. I poured some into a glass with ice and took a sip. Whiskey. Together with Mahmoud, a hefty middle-aged businessman from Tehran, we drank the can dry.

The apartment had track lighting, modern appliances and furniture, but we all sat around on the living room floor. Aref's brother looked up at his wife and smiled.

"Her name means 'A person who has freedom,'" he said. "She was born in 1979, when people thought the revolution was a good thing." He paused to take a sip of wine. "Little did we know that it was the worst revolution in the world."

Turning to me, he asked what I thought of Iran, but he refused to accept my stock answer – that the people are wonderful and hospitable, the land is beautiful – he wanted to go deeper.

"What do the common people in Canada think of Iran, people who have not visited? We watch the same satellite television. We see the lies they tell," he said sharply.

"I think most people can recognize the difference between a government and a people," I said.

"But what of the news?" he pressed.

"Well, it's a problem," I admitted. "I don't think that Western news agencies lie, exactly. They just focus on a certain angle of a story. Every agency does that. We should probably watch several stations for a more balanced view." We should filter through all the news stations and visit every country for ourselves, conducting original research, speaking with locals, journalists, politicians, scientists, and theologians. Except no one has time for that.

"What will you tell people about us when you return to Canada?"

"Just what I told you, that the people are friendly. Also, that not everyone supports the government. They want change, but they also want peace."

Aref's brother raised his glass. "You are welcome in my house," he said.

Still carrying the warm glow of whiskey to fend off the night chill, Aref, Mahmoud, and I arrived at the station. Steam poured from beneath the black train as we hurried on board to get out of the sleet. As we got under way, I lay in the top bunk with my head next to the open window. It was hot in the cabin. I smiled as the cool spray from the snow outside touched my face. Eventually I fell asleep to the rhythm of the train.

My flight from Tehran to Damascus was cancelled several days in a row because of heavy snowfall. I had already made the trip to the airport twice, and the weather didn't look any better on this day, but I decided to try again. As the taxi driver left city limits, the road conditions deteriorated. Having deviated from the beaten path, a tractor now spun its wheels in soft snow along the shoulder. The few taxis still operating crawled along slippery roads layered with packed snow.

The world grew dark as we inched closer to the airport. I scanned the sky. No aircraft landing lights. They would cancel my flight again. I could feel it. Then, just a kilometre away from the airport, a bright white spot grew in the fog as one lumbering airplane dropped into view. I turned to my driver and smiled.

None of the monitors in the departures area displayed any information. They were all blacked out. An impatient crowd vented their frustration. There was shouting. A few angry travellers cornered airport employees, screaming at them to make airplanes materialize through the fog. That seemed effective, actually. They succeeded in coercing staff to open the check-in counters. Now we could collect our boarding passes, but it had no influence on whether or not airplanes could land.

Clutching my pass, I asked a lady in line if she thought the plane would fly.

"It will fly," she said, "inshallah."

They delayed the flight again and again, until most of us waiting had given up hope. Surely the plane would not arrive, we thought. Or if it did, it would not take off again. But, five hours after our scheduled departure for Damascus, I buckled myself into a seat at the very back of the aircraft. I once read that passengers farthest aft stand the best chance of surviving a crash.

Looking out the window as we taxied out, I could see thick frost on the wings. Piles of snow lined the runway. Taking note of the nearest emergency exit, I cinched the seatbelt tight against my hips.

After all that, there was no drama on the flight at all. The plane touched down in Damascus at 3:00 a.m. and a taxi brought me to within a few blocks of the hotel. I knew the area. It would be easier for me to walk from there than to guide the driver in any farther. Stepping out into the night, my body carried me along familiar roads, over a pedestrian bridge, and past a fountain with the inscription, "Always Remember God."

When I arrived at the front door, the hotel was locked. I cupped my hands against the window to peer inside. Someone was sleeping on the floor by the front desk. I rapped on the glass. No movement. When I rang the bell, the person on the floor stirred to life. It was Harley. Wiping the sleep from his eyes, he let me in and showed me to a room.

Dropping my pack on the bed, I hurried downstairs. I passed through the main courtyard before feeling my way along the dark hallway towards the rear of the building. Reaching blindly, I located the door that opened onto the backyard where I had left the Oscillator.

I shivered, stopping to take a deep breath. This was the moment that I had been waiting for. During my entire stay in Iran, the Oscillator remained in my thoughts. On every uncomfortable bus journey, with each delay at a station or

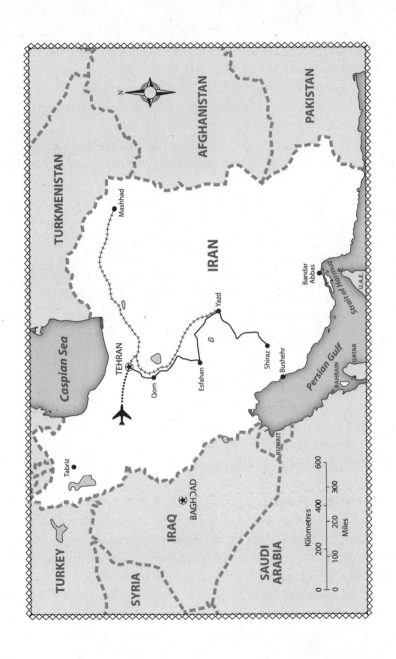

failed attempt to figure out a departure schedule, I longed for the bike. I worried about it, too. It was so far away. In quiet moments I wondered if I would ever see the machine again. It felt like a lifeline that somehow connected me to my home, and I had let go.

I pushed the door open slowly, like a father checking on a sleeping child. I held my breath. Only when I could look in on the yard did I exhale.

There it was: the Oscillator. It had a ghostly glow about it in the moonlight, all silver and grey. A kafiya hung from the wing mirror. I had never seen it look more beautiful.

Under closer examination, the machine had a film of cement dust on every surface. That accounted to some degree for its pallid appearance. Someone had moved it. With the steering and both wheels locked in position, they must have dragged it. By scuff marks on the ground and a foot peg folded up, I could tell that it had been dropped. Basically, though, the machine seemed fine.

"It looks like we've both had an adventure while I was gone," I whispered, patting the gas tank. Brushing off the dust from the seat, I climbed into the saddle. I clicked on the lights to check the battery, but I resisted the urge to start it up right then and there. That could wait until morning.

I stayed in Damascus for the next week with two new friends who I met at the hostel. Travis was a part-time archaeologist from the States who had just finished touring Europe as the drummer for a heavy metal band, though with his short red hair and neat beard, I never would have guessed that.

Looking at Amanda, I never would have guessed her occupation, either. A slender brunette with bright eyes, long lashes and a pretty smile, Amanda worked as a freelance journalist specializing in conflict zones. She was in Damascus organizing her papers for Iraq. As it turned out, we were both from the same part of Alberta.

Though disparate souls, the three of us clicked right away, spending most of our waking hours together smoking narghile, wandering the old city, or hanging out in coffee shops. We discussed travel plans. Together, Amanda and I convinced Travis that he should visit Lebanon. It was safe, we assured him. Within a few days of his arrival in Beirut, a car bomb exploded just a few blocks from Travis and someone stole nearly everything he had. He claims to have enjoyed the visit all the same.

Amanda got her Iraqi papers soon after Travis left for Lebanon. She would fly into Baghdad in a few days, leaving me without a friend in Damascus. That settled it. It was time for me to move on.

CONCLUSION

After sorting through my gear the next morning, I ended up with a pile of business cards for hostels and scrap bits of paper with phone numbers on them. I threw them all away. Organizing everything took time. I had been living out of my backpack for so long that I had trouble remembering where things belonged in my motorcycle luggage. It would take a few days of riding before it would become routine again.

Amanda and I went out for breakfast, but we didn't speak very much. In fact, we didn't speak very much at all that entire morning. Returning to the hotel, she quietly watched me fumble with straps and buckles while loading the bike. I gathered the last of my things from the room as Amanda looked on. When I had neatly tucked everything away, we sat down in the courtyard. She handed me a cigarette.

All dressed up in my motorcycle gear, I walked out to the Oscillator. To avoid a long goodbye with Amanda, I started the engine right away. Then we embraced. We had only known each other for a few days, but bonds develop quickly between travellers. A lump formed in my throat. I was getting sick of goodbyes – perhaps another indication that I should go home.

We held each other for what seemed like a long time. As she pressed against me, I could feel her warmth even through our jackets. She had a pleasant smell of vanilla and bubble gum. When we pulled away, there was a moment where I wanted to kiss her. Instead, I put on my helmet. I might not have total control over my emotions, but I could control how I responded to them. It was easier in the daytime.

"I really will miss you," I said.

On the bike, I rolled slowly out of the parking lot, turning to wave at the last moment. Amanda stood with her feet together, head held high, smiling and waving back. Her long black coat was cinched against her waist. Sunlight glinted off her gold hoop earrings.

As I entered the flow of traffic, my head buzzed with nicotine and mixed emotions. It felt good to ride again, but awkward, too. Hands and feet stabbed at controls. Once I even shifted by mistake without the clutch, swearing inside my helmet. I stared straight ahead rather than shoulder-checking or watching my mirrors. The bike did not feel like an extension of me at that point.

I pulled over after a few blocks to adjust my gloves. Farther on, I stopped to put on sunglasses. Things were coming back to me now. I moved through traffic with greater confidence every minute. Leaving the city, I rode with an open visor, enjoying the cool air on my face.

Soon I found a smooth road leading south through a landscape of boulders and sand. The road stretched out before me as though someone had snapped it down with a chalk line. Whoever built it knew where they wanted it to go, although I could not tell where it would take me. Oh, I knew that it pointed south into Jordan. Beyond that, Africa hung from it like a plumb bob, but between here and there the road would turn. It would fork eventually and, at that point, I would have to choose a direction based on incomplete information.

That seemed like a better way to travel, to choose the path

as it unfolds rather than trying to force a way through to a preconceived destination. If I followed the road long enough it would wind through differing landscapes, cultures, and political climates. It would curve around a body of water that mixed somehow with the distant Maritsa River that stood between Europe and the Middle East. I would encounter people who practiced strange traditions. They would have their own superstitions, their own mythology. I would find people who had outgrown God, and others who sought him using unfamiliar religious systems.

It's not their fault. It's not my fault that I've always searched for God through the lens of Christianity. Faith and culture are inseparable. How I view God is shaped by where I was born. In most cases, the culture chooses for us the religious texts we read. It shapes our interpretation of the text. To a large degree, it influences how much time we have to consider spiritual matters. If I struggle every day to sift through a mountain of garbage for scrap cardboard, I may not do a proper dissection of anything I read, for example. If I had grown up in Mashhad, Beirut, Istanbul, or Damascus, I would have developed a different picture of the Divine.

I like to think, though, that I would still consider God. And I hope that, given the luxury of time, I would occasionally step back to look at the lens.

That was it. If someone asked me now why I had wanted to go to Iran I would have a more complete answer. Though I had failed to see it earlier, part of the motivation was to search out God from another vantage point. Ultimately, it was that search that led me to Mashhad.

In Mashhad that night, it felt as though God had visited me in the hotel room. In the morning, that notion faded. Even cursory online research provided a medical explanation.

It was nothing serious. Still, just because I can explain something doesn't mean that God didn't do it.

What did I know? Not very much, I'm afraid. All my life I've sought God through a lens, as we all do, but it's a long lens. Through it, you just can't see everything. I decided that I should pray more often, even if no one hears me. I discovered that the thread of hope I had for God was thin, but that it was also strong. The next time someone asked me if I was a Christian, I would say, "Yes, inshallah."

That said, I knew that I would always have doubts, right to the very last. If only I keep riding I will eventually face the same fears as I did in Iran. But who knows? Perhaps on one of these occasions God will speak clearly. And that frightens me, too.

JEREMY KROEKER is a freelance writer, a speaker, mountaineer and the award-winning author of *Motorcycle Therapy—A Canadian Adventure in Central America*. With his motorcycle, he has travelled to nearly thirty countries while managing to do at least one outrageously stupid thing in every one. He has evaded police in Egypt, tasted tear gas in Israel, scrambled through minefields in Bosnia and Lebanon, and wrangled a venomous snake in Austria. One time he got a sliver in El Salvador. His writing has appeared in newspapers such as the *Toronto Star, Winnipeg Free Press*, and *Calgary Herald*, and in US magazines such as *Alpinist* and *Outrider Journal*. He was born in Manitoba, grew up in Saskatchewan and currently lives in Canmore, Alberta.